PRACTICING SUCCESSFULLY
A Masterclass in the Musical Art

PRACTICING
SUCCESSFULLY

A Masterclass in the Musical Art

Elizabeth A. H. Green

GIA Publications, Inc.
Chicago

Book layout and design: Martha Chlipala
Copy editor: Elizabeth Dallman Bentley
Music engraving: Paul Burrucker

Photograph on page 7 courtesy of the Bentley Historical Library,
University of Michigan, Michigan Daily records, Box 19. Used with
permission.

G-6646
ISBN: 1-57999-510-1

GIA Publications, Inc.
7404 South Mason Avenue, Chicago 60638
www.giamusic.com

Printed in the United States of America

CONTENTS

To the Reader: On Using This Book 5

Reflections on Elizabeth A. H. Green by Rebecca Ericsson Hunter . . 7

Foreword by E. Daniel Long 11

Introduction by H. Robert Reynolds 13

Prelude 15

Part One: The Practicing

Chapter One
Defeating Monotony with the Rhythmic Motif 19

Chapter Two
Practicing in Threes: Broadening the View 27

Chapter Three
Practicing in Fours: The Four-Note Motifs 35

Chapter Four
Practicing with Cross Accentuation: Developing New Challenges . 41

Chapter Five
Practicing Sequences, Scales, and Accentuations
    (Substitution Accents) 47

Chapter Six
Practicing Modern Innovations: The Missing Technique 55

Chapter Seven
Practicing the Etudes: The Lengthened Attention Span 59

Chapter Eight
Practicing Sight-Reading: Why You Can't Sight-Read Easily 65

Chapter Nine
Practicing the Piano—A Stringed Instrument: Its Uniqueness 73

Chapter Ten
Practicing Double-Stops and Chords: For the Bowed Strings 79

Part Two: The Instruments as Professionals See Them

Chapter Eleven
The Woodwinds: Flute, Oboe, Clarinet, Saxophone, Bassoon 87

Chapter Twelve
The Brasses: French Horn, Trumpet (Cornet),
   Trombone, Tuba (Euphonium) 97

Chapter Thirteen
The Strings: Violin, Viola, Cello, String Bass 105

Part Three: Science and Teaching

Chapter Fourteen
The Brain and the Learning Process 117

Chapter Fifteen
Introducing the Child to Serious Practice 121

Chapter Sixteen
Summary on Teaching 127

The Experts 131

Acknowledgments 139

Bibliography 141

About the Author 143

Comprehensive Index 145

To the Reader:
On Using This Book

Sir or Madam:

You have picked up this book because you are a person who practices. A quick glance at the Contents leaves no doubt that practicing *is* discussed.

Because you have practiced, you have already experienced the *monotony of unvaried repetition*. You may also have experienced the phenomenon of the repetitions continuing unabated while the mind roams at large elsewhere.

A good practice method must, therefore, accomplish two things: it must add an efficient variety to the repetitions in order to capture your interest, and it must force the mind to concentrate (see Chapters One through Ten).

A fundamental change occurred during the second half of the twentieth century. The earthshaking impact of the brain research since the mid-twentieth century has made us all conscious of the brain in a way we never have been before. The *link* from the brain (the thought in the mind) to the response in the hands (the technique) has been clarified through an understanding of how that "link" functions. It is called the "neural pathway" (see Chapter Fourteen).

In order to make this book practical for winds, strings, and piano, comparisons and differences are mentioned frequently throughout.

Part Two is given over entirely to the instruments themselves. To make the book functional for readers who are not personally familiar with each of the instruments, certain information of a basic nature is supplied in a unique way.

Each instrument is discussed by an outstanding professional performer who has also been recognized as an equally outstanding teacher. Names and titles are listed alphabetically in the back of the book.

These authorities answer two questions of a primary nature: 1) What are the distinctive features of your instrument that make it unique? and 2) What is the most basic teaching of that instrument?

The reader is urged to peruse the material of Part Two (every word of it!).

There is an ever-present temptation to read only the sections dealing with one's own field of specialization. But here it is gently suggested that rich dividends may accrue by broadening the horizon and taking advantage of this opportunity to make comparisons.

In the process of exploring the ins and outs of the less familiar instruments, the reader may be startled by an unexpected flash of insight demanding experimentation on his own instrument (performing or teaching).

In Part Three, a few additions are made to the teaching principles exemplified in the text throughout, together with ideas on training the young student to *practice successfully*.

—Elizabeth A. H. Green
June 1995

Reflections on Elizabeth A. H. Green

Elizabeth A. H. Green's introduction to music came early. Her mother, Mary, (my great aunt) played songs on the piano to entertain her baby daughter. Her father, Albert, focused on developing her ear for music readiness. When Elizabeth cried, which was only occasionally, he comforted her and played a pitch on the piano; she learned to cry on pitch!

Albert, who taught violin professionally, began teaching Elizabeth on a quarter-size instrument when she was four years old. She progressed rapidly. At age five she gave her first recital in a church parlor before an audience of one hundred. So entranced was she by the concept of an audience—smiling faces focused solely on her—that she gazed out in wonder at the audience as she played, not looking at her music, which she had memorized and knew perfectly. Yet there came a time in the recital when she wished to find her place in the score and, when she did not immediately locate it, called out, "Papa, come here quick!" By the time he had reached the stage, however, she had already found her place and never missed a beat.

Elizabeth and my mother, Florence, were first cousins, but they were as close as sisters. Visits from Elizabeth were eagerly anticipated and guaranteed laughter and merriment. She had a lively mind and a ready sense of humor, but more than that she was a loving presence in my life for four generations of our family. I treasure times spent with her, whether celebrating milestones or, as important, embracing the everyday components of life that bring contentment. She never lost sight of the beauty and wonders of the world around her. She never stopped learning. Her extraordinary facility in teaching made her a gifted and effective educator. She championed goals that nurtured growth and inspired one's best effort. She led her life with confidence, energy, and panache.

Elizabeth was often asked what the initials A. H. stood for in her name. With a twinkle in her eye, her standard reply was, "And How." In truth, the A is for Adine, a violin student of her father's, the H for Herkimer. General Nicholas Herkimer, an ancestor of Elizabeth's and mine, was in charge of the Battle of Oriskany, New York, one of the turning points of the Revolutionary War. This was not far from where her mother and my grandmother (who were Timmermans) were later born and grew up. One of the Herkimer soldiers was Lieutenant Henry Timmerman, another ancestor of ours. In that battle, Timmerman was scalped and left for dead. Herkimer was wounded and commanded the battle sitting in his saddle, which had been pulled off his horse and placed beneath a tree so he could lean against its trunk. At battle's end Herkimer had Timmerman brought with him to Herkimer's home where both men were given first aid. Timmerman survived; Herkimer did not. From Herkimer, Elizabeth inherited a name, from Herkimer and Timmerman, she inherited spirit, faith, and independence. And How.

Her ability to inspire the best in musicians was notable. In Ann Arbor at a concert dedicated to her memory, a guest conductor shared with the audience an anecdote about Elizabeth. Most conductors compliment their orchestras after a performance by saying, "That was great." Elizabeth would say, "That was great; now how can we make it better?" She expected the best, inspired those around her to excel, and encouraged them to do so.

In many ways this book was Elizabeth's final gift to music education. It was written over a period of years. While the book was in progress, Elizabeth was diagnosed with cancer. She consulted with her physicians, assessed the situation, and weighed the alternatives. After consideration, she declined any treatment, writing one letter to her doctors, and a second one to me to explain her rationale. She simply chose to finish the book without compromising her intellect, which she feared might have been a side effect of treatment.

As it was, work on the book became increasingly arduous. She would write for two hours, lie down for one, and then repeat. Never one to relinquish a goal once set, she persevered until the book's completion with a determination few could muster. At the same time she renewed her knowledge of the Russian language as a mental exercise and kept a notebook nearby for practice. Indeed, she was writing notes to herself in Russian the week before she died. (Russian was just one of the half dozen languages in which she was conversant. In fact, when invited to speak in a foreign country she did, when appropriate, deliver her address in the native language.)

Elizabeth A. H. Green was revered and cherished by peers and students alike. Strong of faith and firm in her convictions, she enriched the lives of others far beyond the scope of music. This book stands as a testament to her dedication to music, her diligence in the pursuit of excellence, her joy in sharing her knowledge, and, above all, her love of life and love of learning.

In closing her home in Ann Arbor, I found several dozen ballpoint pens which she had had imprinted with the admonition "Know the Score." Indeed, this was a woman who absolutely knew the score, never missed a beat, and was gracious enough to teach the rest of us. Thank you Elizabeth Green—And How.

—Rebecca Ericsson Hunter

Foreword

"You must practice what you preach." How many times have we heard that statement made regarding effective teaching? One of the many characteristics often associated with fine teachers is that they never stop learning. Another quality of the best teachers is that they spend extra time studying scores, "practicing" if you will, until they have mastered the part before going into the classroom.

In this book Elizabeth Green takes an approach that reverses this often-used phrase. "Practice what you preach" becomes "Preach what you practice."

Although Green's idea to write a book about practicing had been germinating for some time, a personal experience led her to begin to put her thoughts down on paper in earnest. Always one to stay physically and mentally fit, she had been an active walker all her life. On one of her frequent walks about the neighborhood, she tripped and fell, fracturing one of her arms. The recovery involved several weeks of immobility with her arm in a cast and sling.

When the day finally arrived for the cast to come off ("Hallelujah!" she exclaimed), Elizabeth's first desire was to immediately begin practicing. She was eager to play and wanted to begin honing her playing skills, something she had not done for many weeks.

To her dismay, her eighty-something-year-old arm and fingers would not do what she expected on her violin. Being an individual not easily deterred, she had the idea that maybe it would be easier to first begin on her viola. She thought because the space between the fingers is greater she would have an easier time doing her exercises. No such luck. It was just too difficult.

Determined to find a way to get her joints flexible and moving, Miss Green, as she was afectionately called by all her students, decided to see what would happen if she attempted to play a double bass. She went to

11

the University of Michigan School of Music. (Having the rank of professor emeritus has its advantages.) Sure enough, she checked out a bass, and off she went. While standing with her right arm extended, she was able to play two- and three-note exercises. Some time later she switched to her violin and continued on the road to rehabilitation. Thus began the slow, steady process of learning from the very beginning the art of "practicing successfully."

Elizabeth A. H. Green was a pioneer in the field of music and conducting and a major force in the development of string education. During the last few months of her life she not only completed this book but also finished the sixth edition of *The Modern Conductor*. Now in its seventh printing, this book remains a standard text in many conducting classes throughout the United States and beyond. She accomplished in her last year what most do not do in a lifetime.

The music world suffered a great loss when Elizabeth Green died. She had a profound impact on those of us who were fortunate enough to have her as a mentor, teacher, and friend. She was most generous with her knowledge and expertise. It is our good fortune that she left behind a wide collection of material. Through numerous articles and books dealing with a wide range of musical topics, her legacy lives on. With the addition of this book, we can add one more resource from this amazing woman to our musical libraries.

It is interesting to note that although most of her writing dealt with orchestras, music education, and string pedagogy, she wrote her last book for everyone. This volume can be used by all players of all instruments and by all teachers—it is a book for all musicians.

Her last printed words focus on an assignment she gave to herself, the same one she had given thousands of times to others: PRACTICING SUCCESSFULLY.

She did practice what she preached—she preached how to practice. Amen!

—E. Daniel Long
Ann Arbor Public Schools, retired
Ann Arbor, Michigan
July 2005

Introduction

It was my great honor and pleasure to be a student of Elizabeth Green's. Such a privilege was valued by thousands who learned from her at the University of Michigan, as I did, and by those in scores of clinics she gave throughout the country. Her books on conducting and string pedagogy set the standard by which other texts are judged, and her influence on the conducting profession is, in my opinion, greater than any other teacher of this craft.

Elizabeth Green lived for teaching; if anyone showed a desire to learn, she was there to teach. Teaching was what she loved. She came to life in front of a class of young musicians, and she infected the room with enthusiasm whether those in attendance were gifted and advanced or just beginners. What she offered was keen insight into what constituted the craft of conducting and teaching. The smallest details were cherished techniques, and the sum of these seemingly infinitesimal aspects came together in a technical mastery that she communicated with joy and effervescence. She not only could teach it, she could **do it**.

To be in her class was a great privilege, and, remarkable as it seems, those of us who had that privilege knew how significant it was at the time. When asking anyone who had been a student of Elizabeth Green's, "Who was the greatest teacher you ever had?" the universal and immediate answer is: "Elizabeth Green." This answer never changes.

While we all had many great and famous teachers, she remains the standard of excellence to all who knew her and learned from her.

In reading and studying her books, you can feel her presence. She dedicated herself to the presentation of important techniques in order to present her conclusions so that others would benefit from her dedicated study.

This book on practicing is no exception to her dedication and self-sacrifice. Sometime before finishing this book, she was diagnosed with cancer. Drugs were prescribed to delay the inevitable, but she refused to take them because, she said, "They might dull my mind so that I could not finish the book." During this time of great anguish for her, I visited her both in the hospital and at her home. She was always full of life and talked with great enthusiasm about her book and its progress.

So many years after being a formal student of hers (I will, in fact, always be her student), I still find myself remembering her lessons in music and in life. Her influence on the lives she touched is never muted, and those of us who had the great privilege of studying with and knowing her have always felt truly blessed.

—H. Robert Reynolds
Student and friend of Elizabeth Green
Director emeritus of University of
Michigan Bands
Principal wind ensemble conductor,
University of Southern California

Prelude

The summer session was well underway at a famous university that evening in 1933 when this incident took place.

Fiddles in hand, a fellow student and I slipped into one of the basement practice rooms to check on several difficult passages before the evening's rehearsal. Propping the music up on the stand, we began practicing.

About twenty minutes into the hour, this serious effort to attain perfection was rudely interrupted by the equally serious efforts of a pianist next door. Someone was belaboring a frustrating run that started below middle C and galloped upward for several octaves, both hands cooperating on the passage. When he arrived at a certain spot in the third octave, his fingers tangled, forcing him to stop.

How many times this had happened before it thrust itself upon our consciousness we never knew. But each time the pianist fumbled, he started back at the beginning of the run only to break down again at the same place.

Further, he was practicing at full tempo. Never once did he isolate the offending notes, play them slowly, find out how the passage should *sound*, and locate which notes were causing the trouble.

After another dozen failures, the frustration increased. His playing became louder, the speed more frantic. Finally: the breaking point! In sheer desperation, two clenched fists came down on the keyboard with a magnificent crash that all but sent the ivories flying off into space. Silence! *Prolonged and heavenly silence!*

Then a door slammed, and footsteps faded into oblivion.

What a staggering sum, in trillions of hours, the devotees of music must have employed during the centuries as they impatiently drove their skills toward a perfection that seldom arrived!

Those among us who are eternally enticed by this elusive art soon learn that *music* is a demanding goddess. The worshipper sets goals. But regardless of what the goals may be, and regardless of what amount of God-given talent he or she may have, ultimate success depends upon one immutable, inescapable, and well-publicized fact: the musician has to practice—successfully or not.

PART ONE:
THE PRACTICING

CHAPTER ONE

Defeating Monotony
with the Rhythmic Motif

Practicing becomes one of life's most frustrating experiences when the hours pile up without positive results. Unproductive practice time can be attributed to several rather common causes:

- The performer's mind is not entirely focused upon the activity.
- The practicing is too, too, too fast, allowing mistakes to happen. A cycle of mistake correction, repeated a number of times during the practice hour, is habit forming.
- Good basic practice habits have not been taught early enough in the learning process.

There is a certain art to effective practicing, and there are fundamental principles to be understood and applied. Practicing can take many forms, but the activity itself begins with drudgery, slowly passes through stages of depression, moves to hopefulness and genuine interest, and finally comes to inspired commitment, a daily adventure.

Practicing is an adult activity. It takes mature determination. No wonder children view it with little enthusiasm! Practicing forces them to act in a grown-up manner—these young people who are full of excitement, of the spirit of motion itself, as they dash full speed ahead.

Practicing puts a harness on all of that. Why? Because practicing is essentially a monotonous repetition. But it doesn't have to be.

The first successful antidote to monotony is variety. Variety creates interest. Interest creates attention. Attention means that the senses (ears and eyes) are working and that the mind is focused, full power, on what is taking place.

When practicing arrives at the state of fascinated attention, the passing of time is no longer part of our consciousness. We have migrated to a different world—a higher plateau with an expanding view.

So this book explores variety in all of its connotations. A different path sometimes turns into a shortcut. Even so, at its least attractive moments, the view is new and different.

The rhythmic motif furnishes great variety—when to use it, how to apply it. First, we encounter these motifs in less demanding forms and, later on, in various levels of difficulty. In the process, we shall discover a certain development has taken place. In the eyes (sight), then in the ears (hearing), and finally in the mind, the rhythmic motif can solve the almost endless challenges presented by this manner of practicing. It should be a stimulating experience.

The simplest form of music is tone applied to a single pitch. Most basic in the technique of any instrument is *tone*. We explore it in all of its majesty: its personal qualities and its dynamic coloring, even if only on one note. Here, however, we are interested in the relationship between two or more sounds.

The smallest musical motif is comprised of only two pitches, an intervallic relationship. Beethoven chose a two-note motif for the opening notes of his Fifth Symphony. And he pursued it in his two-note rhythmic groupings until the last movement when the triad bursts forth in all its glory.

The simplest rhythmic figure, for our purposes, is also comprised of two notes: the dotted-eighth sixteenth. It provides instant variety because it can be reversed to sixteenth plus dotted eighth, thus giving an entirely different way to render the succession of notes (see Example 1).

EXAMPLE 1. The dotted-eighth sixteenth

The passage as it appears in the music:

The first application:

The second application:

Practicing with this particular rhythm forces the mind and eyes to prepare two notes at a time, the fast sixteenth and the dotted eighth that follows immediately.

When the fingers tangle while reading a difficult passage (a "run" or a series of "impossible" measures), it is time to choose a suitable practice rhythm. Fingers can tangle on the piano, the woodwinds, and the stringed instruments, but difficulties are less obvious on the brasses where three fingers on a hand can manage nicely.

In the following passage, the accidentals alone can cause enough trouble. Certain players invariably use rhythmic practice to conquer it (see Example 2).

EXAMPLE 2. Concerto for Clarinet and Orchestra in A, op. 57, by Carl Nielsen

(A) Conquer the passage with both applications in Example 1.

(B) A typical technical training passage
(horn, woodwind, strings, piano)

There is a logical order for applying the practice rhythms. The first step is absolutely imperative:

1. Play the passage through *very slowly*, sustaining each note until the ear has it firmly in mind. (Strings should use separate bows with no slurs.) *Nothing can be gained from rhythmic practice until the ear has first clearly established the sequence of the notes.*

2. Apply the first rhythm, and repeat until you can play the passage with ease. This rhythm speeds the transition between notes two and three.

3. Reverse the rhythm to add speed between the first pair of notes.

The dotted-eighth sixteenth is usually the first choice because it has been around a long time and is quoted in many books. Try it, even if the troublesome passage is in triplets. What you are doing first is establishing the *note sequence* regardless of the original rhythmic setting.

There is still one more step to be taken for security. The conquered passage is not fully learned until it is reinserted into the composition and clamped into place with what precedes and follows it. It may be necessary to use the practice rhythms throughout the clamping process. You now have the general outline for applying rhythms to any difficult passage.

This type of practice focuses the attention because two notes must be prepared (read) ahead. This is the first step in what becomes a lengthy period of mental development. The time eventually arrives when the demands of the more difficult practice rhythms cannot be met unless the mental processes have likewise kept pace.

Finally, of premium importance, using rhythmic motifs can bring the student to the "threshold of discovery." The following remark has been heard more than once: "During my practice time I seem to be discovering things I had never noticed before." (Hallelujah!)

The rhythmic motif as a practice device: The use of the rhythmic motif as a practice device solves one eternal problem for the teacher: it slows down the student's practicing and forces the student to look at each note consciously and to group notes into combinations that are not printed on the page.

EXAMPLE 3. Space beats evenly throughout

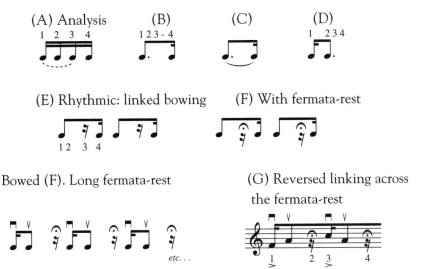

The dotted-eighth sixteenth is recognized rather universally as the basic motif (if any) to be applied. These two little notes, so often carelessly performed as a triplet, seem to have a special quality. They can be reiterated on a single pitch just to perfect their own accuracy, or they can be applied as shown in Example 3.

The first step is to drill the accurate rhythmic performance of each pair. Letter B, unslurred, becomes an articulation study. Letter C, slurred, is good for a series of repeated scale tones. D reverses the figure to conquer the passages in a new way.

At E, the addition of the sixteenth rest pushes precision still further. Take a slow tempo, speaking the "one, two, stop, four" very evenly and paying attention to the exact length of the notes.

In applying any of the rhythms, as in F or later on, the fermata-rest comes after the long note. The stop can be as long as necessary to prepare the next two notes. *Mistakes are not allowed when the fermata-rest is used.* Its main purpose is to prevent mistakes from happening. *It provides time for the mind to think.* Once the mind is secure in what the next two notes actually are, they are then played as fast as possible. This is where speed begins its development.

The first practice step is to play the troublesome passage slowly, listening to every note. The note sequence is inviolate. The ear must hear it accurately several times before any rhythmic patterns are applied.

In application, the first written note matches the first note of the rhythmic pattern; the second written note is the next note of the pattern as applied.

Using the reversed form, D, speed is created between the first two notes. Actually, the speed of iteration is greater than the player will need when the passage is reinserted into the composition. Ultimately, both accuracy and speed have been securely mastered when the rhythm is again inserted. When accuracy is achieved, it is not so difficult to play rhythmically.

It is imperative that the reinsertion of the passage into the composition be well practiced using several measures before and after the practiced passage.

This rhythmic pattern can be applied to an entire passage. Applied to any series of notes (regardless of the original rhythm), conquering the series with both forms of the pattern will build finger accuracy and ultimately more speed than actually needed.

For perfect results, start with the fermata-rest inserted. Allow the fermata-rest to govern. No mistakes, *not even one*, are permitted when practicing this way. Take enough time to get it right every time. Slow down the overall speed. Discard the fermata-rest when it is no longer needed.

The greatest benefit of all from the use of the fermata-rest is that the fast motion of the fingers is immediately followed by relaxation. Speed is built without constant muscular tension.

For the advanced player, the fermata-rest can be used rhythmically with the fast fingering coming immediately after the rest.

When accuracy has been achieved in the mind, the two notes following the fermata-rest are played as rapidly as possible. Then the next fermata-rest is used to prepare for the next pair of notes. The stop can be as long as necessary to ensure accuracy. Gradually, as skill matures, the fermata-rest disappears. Note: In this rhythm and in the difficult rhythms to be encountered in the following chapters, the fermata-rest (when used) occurs after the long note and before the fast notes. For complete mastery, each passage must be conquered using both parts of Example 4.

EXAMPLE 4. Use of the fermata-rest in difficult rhythms

EXAMPLE 5. Some typical passages

Strings: *Francesca da Rimini*, op. 32, by Piotr Tchaikovsky

Brasses: *Pictures at an Exhibition*, "The Great Gate of Kiev,"
by Modest Mussorgsky, arr. Maurice Ravel

Woodwinds: *La Mer* by Claude Debussy

Chapter Two

Practicing in Threes: Broadening the View

There are certain facets of music performance that are common to all of us regardless of our choice of instrument. Except for the brasses, we use both of our hands in the process of turning the printed score into audible sound. For woodwind players and pianists, the fingers are note-conscious. But the pianist and the harpist are the only ones whose fingers actually make the notes *sound*. The rest of us turn to some other medium for creating the tone: a stream of breath for the winds and a bow for the strings. (The bow gets gradually shorter as the stringed instrument gets gradually longer.)

In addition, the bow needs rosin to make a sound, the clarinets and saxophones need a reed, and the oboes, English horn, and bassoon use a double reed. The only thing needed by the trombonist, in addition to the usual wind, lips, and mouthpiece, is a long right arm.

So here we stand, all of us, a motley crowd with our varied techniques, our preferences, our musical opinions, and, yes, our prejudices.

Fortunately there is one immutable thing that forces us to cooperate and ultimately to agree: the RHYTHM. It completely ignores our individuality. Rhythm is the one universal technique, so it is universally applicable as a practice device.

In Chapter One we dealt with the interval, a two-note relationship and a two-note practice motif. Now, as we add a third note to the group, we discover an anomaly: a two-beat motif can be adapted beautifully to a three-note (triplet) grouping. The first two motifs in Example 6 are comprised of two units: one long note plus a pair of short notes that are equal in value to the long note. This brings a faint suggestion of hemiola (cross accentuation). But the given motifs still preserve the basic three-note accent of the original excerpts. They are adaptable to three-note groupings for any instrument. This type of crossover becomes challenging as the difficulty of the motifs increases.

Example 6 shows a two-beat unit in A and B adapted to the three-note grouping. (Note: the fermata-rest is customarily not needed in this case.)

EXAMPLE 6. Two-beat unit adapted to a three-note grouping

Treble clef, violin: *Fantasia Appassionata*, op. 35, by Henri Vieuxtemps

Bass clef, cello: *Tarantella*, op. 23, by William Squire

| (A) Highlights | (B) Highlights | (C) Highlights |
| the first note | the last note | the middle note |

With the addition of the third note, the *aspect* changes. The rhythmic motif as shown highlights each note of the composer's sequence, giving a subtle security to the ear as the sequence progresses. Each variation (A, B, or C) should be practiced and conquered *individually* on whatever passage is being perfected. These rhythms are much easier than the dotted-eighth sixteenth.

As the practice progresses, listen for dynamic unity in A and B throughout the three notes. There is an ever-present danger that dynamic disunity may unconsciously occur. Build the skill first. Later, musical variation can be added as the passage requires.

Winds: All wind players spend a good amount of practice time improving the long tone combined with *crescendo* and *diminuendo*. When the basic dynamic control is good, then apply the dynamic changes to these motifs at a slow tempo. The two sixteenths can either lead toward a *forte* climax or become a first step in a long *diminuendo* when ending a slow piece.

EXAMPLE 7. Exercises for practicing dynamic control in the strings

Strings: Choose an etude that is all in steady eighth or sixteenth notes grouped in threes throughout. Apply A and B from Example 6. Use separate bows with no slurs and listen for dynamic evenness. This exercise is especially useful for the orchestral player. When sixteenth notes are played softly by a whole section of violins, the notes do not cut through the rest of the orchestra, especially not in the *fortes*. They are lost to the audience.

Now for Example 8, which uses motif C: this may be the first time some of the younger students have to deal with syncopation. Take an exercise that is in eighth notes or sixteenths and grouped by the composer into threes. Use the bowing as marked and accent the first two notes.

EXAMPLE 8. Use of motif C from Example 6

EXAMPLE 9. Symphony no. 5, op. 64, by Piotr Tchaikovsky

For C-1: Link the final sixteenth to the preceding eighth note (down, up, up). For C-2, measure 2: Lift the bow OFF the string after the first note and take a second down-bow for the accented half note. Pay attention to this. It is the standard orchestral bowing for a syncopated half note in *forte* or louder, unslurred. These two bowings are also good when applied to scale practice.

Have you noticed that you are now preparing the three notes in advance? Sight-reading is being given another subtle urge forward. Use the fermata-rest if you wish. Remember to place it after the longer note each time.

As a sidelight to the relationship of threes and twos, the passage in Example 9 from the second movement of Tchaikovsky's Fifth Symphony is interesting. His brilliant climb to the thrilling climax note (it arrives at quadruple *forte* later in the movement) is so exciting that one is unconscious of the two-note writing in the melody. The musical drive is such that the breadth of two notes per beat is an absolute musical necessity.

Before moving on to the next chapter, let us examine what happens when we apply the dotted-eighth sixteenth to sequences of three notes.

EXAMPLE 10. Applying the dotted-eighth sixteenth to a three-note sequence

Ballet Suite, "Gigue," by André Gretry, arr. Felix Mottl.
(Use B-flat horn for these fingerings.)

Applying the motifs of Chapter One

(A)   (B)

Compared to the strong beats of a 6/8 rhythm, the accent has changed entirely. Each measure is no longer two groups of three notes; it has become three groups of two notes. The time signature itself has undergone a change, becoming 3/4 meter. This matter of accentuation plays a part as we approach the four-note groupings of the next chapter. It also has its place in building facile technique.

The piano: Very little has been said heretofore regarding the piano. The spotlight now shines fully on it as a vehicle to call attention to the variations in difficulty as the rhythmic practice motifs are applied to the different instruments. Certain techniques that are easy for some are difficult for others. Adaptations should be established where necessary, and intelligent choices have to be made. The player's level of technical proficiency dictates the choice.

The pianist and the harpist have a distinction that few of the others of us can match. They use the thumb in each hand as part of their fingering system. (The cellist and the string bass player use the thumb in the upper positions to saddle the string, shortening it.)

Fundamentally, the thumb is placed on the hand to enable us to grasp objects in order to manipulate them. But its wonderful flexibility allows us to align it with the rest of the fingers.

The thumb serves an important place in piano technique because it is shorter than the other fingers and can slip under them to play a note while the hand itself moves throughout the length of the keyboard (see Example 11, the one-octave C scale).

EXAMPLE 11. The one-octave C scale

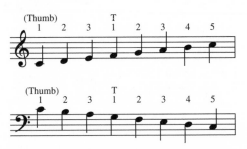

If the first of the motifs for threes is applied, the thumb instantly moves to its position beyond the third finger, ready for the following F.

EXAMPLE 12. Thumb preparation

(A) Fast thumb.   (B) Thumb prepares just the same.

32

Op. 740, Etude no. 2, by Carl Czerny, a difficult arpeggio study for the thumb, trains each hand separately and then together with separate arpeggios (not in octaves). Such a study is impossible if the thumbs are not well trained. The thumbs, together with the third and/or fourth fingers, do not encounter their problems at the same instant. This exercise gives some idea of the difficulties encountered by the pianist. This etude would also be a very effective vehicle for the dotted-eighth sixteenth motifs.

Using the first form of the dotted-eighth sixteenth is a bit easier because there is time to think during the first note and to prepare both fingers and thumb. In either example, the thumb is trained to prepare as soon as it leaves the keyboard.

EXAMPLE 13. Another thumb study

These two are problems in careful timing. The first motif gives the thumb a moment's rest after its preparation due to the longer third-finger note. The second example, with the third finger on the fast note and the thumb's instant play, seems to require just a bit more speed from the thumb.

The fingering system of the piano is the most complex of them all. Each finger is under automatic control. The fingers of the two hands may be playing chords totaling ten notes, or they may be engaged in complicated rhythms that are at variance with each other. But the neurons in the brain accomplish all of this with apparent ease as they form the neural pathways that become habit. When the habit arrives, the musical idea in the mind appears in the hands.

The response of the two hands is equally subtle in the other instruments. Each finger is also under its own control. The fingers needed for the immediate job will activate themselves, separately or together as needed.

What a remarkable structure the human being is! From brain to hands plus the mechanisms of the eyes and ears, all processes coordinate at fantastic speed. And all we have to do is practice until they all work together. We are constructed to be efficient! But we have to pay the price.

---

*For those who are interested in all that is going on in the brain as we perform, *Tone Deaf and All Thumbs? An Invitation to Music Making for Late Bloomers and Non-Prodigies* by neural surgeon Frank R. Wilson (New York: Viking, 1986) is recommended.

Chapter Three

Practicing in Fours: The Four-Note Motifs

As already discovered, rhythmic motifs vary in difficulty as they are applied to the different instruments. Fundamentally, all of us have two techniques: that of producing the sound and that of fingering the note.

The application of rhythmic figures to conquer fingering problems is rather obvious. But they are also useful in tone production. The rhythms speed up the responses of breath, bow control, tongue, and lips just as they do the movement of the fingers.

EXAMPLE 14. Symphony no. 4, Fourth Movement, by Ludwig van Beethoven

Among the most universally effective are the motifs in fours. When the mind concentrates on listening to the quality of sound on the long note and carries it through the ensuing faster notes, the continuity of the passage improves. Phrasal delineation, with its small *crescendos* and *diminuendos*, becomes more unified.

In many instances, there appears to be a tendency to let the speed of the fingering detract from the vitality of the sound. Example 14 presents the basic four-unit rhythmic motif.

As we sight-read, we often recognize patterns in the note sequences. We usually read the patterns successfully without the ear paying any particular attention to the notes *within* the pattern (e.g., short scalar passages and arpeggios).

The four-note motifs of Example 14 build security because they highlight each of the four notes in its proper position within the group.

Patterns A and D give very little trouble as they are applied. But B and C can become annoyingly frustrating, especially as the fast notes cross the normal break between the groups of four. The eyes will easily see the long note. They will resent having to account for the player's tonguing in the middle of the fast notes or the violinist's changing the direction of the bow stroke correspondingly.

The original accentuation on the first note of each four is to be retained when the motifs are applied. The eye-mind response gradually quickens as the practicing continues. The time spent in improving the immediate passage also pays dividends to the overall technical proficiency. This is a doubly effective type of practicing.

EXAMPLE 15. Use of slurs

(A-1) Lip slurs

(B-1) Think in six subdivisions for slow tempo; in three for fast tempo.

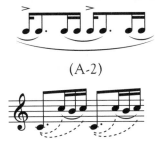

(A-2)

(B-2) Synchronizing tongue and fingers

(C) Breath accent

etc...

(D) Practice each group with *crescendo* and *diminuendo*.

Practiced without slurs, these motifs become an excellent tonguing device. Using the slurs as in C (above), will require a gentle breath accent as the slur arrives on the first note of the following group.

Remember throughout that you are building *control* more than anything else. Be mindful also that in lip-slur reiteration, your success depends upon a clear idea of the sound of the note to which you are moving.

To accent one short note among others is not easy, but this is how you build control. There have been instances in which fine musicians have used the motifs in what they thought was an easier way—moving beat 1 to coincide each time with the long note. This defeats the whole purpose of B and C. The players must realize that the long note in B is the second note of the original passage and that in C it is the third note of the sequence. We are, after all, trying to pay attention to the two middle notes of the passage.

Strings: The following statements may satisfy the curiosity of readers who are but little acquainted with the stringed instruments.

The stringed instruments have certain features that are totally different from any of the other instruments. In addition to the obvious fact that the bow is used to produce the tone, these other factors exist.

While the stringed instrument player uses *both* hands to function on the instrument, the hands are doing two totally different types of work. Yes, the left hand fingers the notes, but it also supports the violin or viola in a manner similar to the woodwinds. For the cello and string bass, the endpin supports the instrument. The left hand's "support" is negligible.

Whereas the woodwind player's hands "stay set," the string player's hands travel the length of the fingerboard. This provides him or her with expanded range on each string and corresponds, in a way, to "alternate fingerings" on the winds. The one advantage for the strings is that the notes do not change pitch as the fingering changes. An A is still an A.

Sliding up and down the fingerboard is similar to the reach of the pianist's hands moving outward from middle C.

The bow has to coordinate with the fingers—their motions synchronize. But the truth of the matter is that the finger has to be ready on the string before the bow can sound it. There is a split second of timing—the difference in movement between the two hands—something of which the player is totally unconscious. It may be only a nanosecond, but this tiny pause does exist.

How do we know this? Because when professional string players type rapidly there are so many errors here and there in the reversal of letter pairs. Instead of "it," the string player types "ti," for example. When this mistake happens in any word, the left-hand letter is invariably typed before the right-hand letter, causing the error.

Bow technique is complicated. For example, there are six different ways to produce a staccato note. Each of these requires a different bow technique "on the string, off the string."

Finally, and completely at odds with the other instruments (except trombone), is the fact that there are no guides to intonation. Placing the correct finger on the correct string guarantees nothing. *The only resource the string player has is his or her own ear.* In this facet, we join the trombone. The French horn player has the crucial problem of hearing the pitch before it is sounded when transposing. Example 16 presents the four-unit motifs with bowing for the stringed instruments.

EXAMPLE 16. Four-unit motifs with bowing

(1) Separate bows. (2) Add rhythmic motifs, one note per bow. (3) For bowing practice, use the bowings as presented.

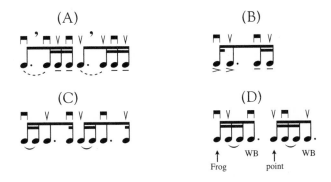

To become utterly secure with a difficult passage of fast notes (all notes of the same metric value), conquer the passage with each of the four motifs *unslurred.* When A is perfect, try B, and so on. Once you become accustomed to working this way, you may find that five times, with each rhythm bowed separately, will perfect most passages, and you will have the notes memorized. With slurs, it becomes a bowing exercise.

The greatest value is that your practice on this one difficult passage also adds to your overall technical proficiency.

The pianist will use the basic form (Example 14A) to conquer difficult runs, each hand individually, then the two together. Later on, the other forms will be explored. Tricky measures, such as those shown in

Example 17, make ideal passages for the motifs of Example 14.

EXAMPLE 17. Op. 740, no. 5, m. 33, by Carl Czerny

Always remember to reinsert the practiced passage into its place in the music and solidify the connections before and after.

CHAPTER FOUR

Practicing with Cross Accentuation: Developing New Challenges

We speak of the art of music. Practicing is also an art. The series of basic practice rhythms presented in the previous chapters can conquer most of the fingering problems of the instrumentalist. But after a period of time, habits form, and the mind ceases to continue its development toward its fullest potential. At this point, new challenges must be initiated. Using the motifs already presented, we apply them in a new way.

Example 18 shows a clumsy passage with skips to unexpected notes. Let us say you have practiced it using the motifs in fours, but it does not feel as if it has become totally easy. What to do?

Try slurring it in threes.

EXAMPLE 18. Passage for using the three-note slur

Suddenly, it is a whole new exercise. It sounds totally different. The accents have redistributed themselves. The ear becomes fascinated by the new aspect of the sounds and the eyes see the notes in a new light. In fact, the eyes must start to *read* the notes again, looking at them one by one.

The reader will notice that the time signature is 4/4. This means there are sixteen notes to the measure. Therefore, the three-note slur moves *through* the barline at the end of the measure. The normal rhythmic accent on the first beat of the measure will not reoccur until the fourth bar begins.

The optional insertion of slurs among unslurred notes can furnish practice challenges similar to the use of rhythmic motifs. Further, a two-note slur in the midst of a long passage of fast staccato tonguing can be a boon to the clarinetist. It will not be noticed by the listener if it is inserted just *before* the accented note: for example, in fours, slur the last two notes of the group because the coming accent makes it less noticeable.

This type of insertion is not necessary for the string player, whose *spiccato* is inexhaustible. Further, a sudden two-note slur will reverse the direction of the bowing and really confuse the issue. The two-note slur, however, is often inserted orchestrally as a link to the last note in a measure in order to arrive on a down-bow on the first note of the following measure.

Another way of using the motifs already learned is in sequence, e.g., two slurred and two separate: reposition the slur in the second group.

EXAMPLE 19. Repositioning the slur

Applying the four-note sequence of Example 14 (p. 35) in sequence is even more difficult.

EXAMPLE 20. Applying the four-note sequence

(A)   (B)

What you are doing in all of these exercises is *building infinite control of your technique.* The mind demands that the fingers obey, and the sight-reading approaches an unshakable perfection.

CAUTION: Do not attempt these difficult problems until you are ready for them. If they create frustration, lay them aside for a month or two until the necessary development has taken place. When they seem "interesting," you are probably ready for them. Try them on a scale or something easy first.

Note-repetition studies are also recommended: Play each note four times. When that is easy, cut to three times, then two times, and finally one time as written. (See also pp. 123–125 in which the four-time reiteration introduces the beginner to serious practice.)

When the speed of one note as written arrives, alternate three and two notes per beat. It makes a fine study for rhythmic precision with a metronome in control. String players will find themselves alternating bows on the accents throughout.

Violin, viola, cello, and string bass: It has been mentioned that as the instruments grow larger the bow grows shorter; it also grows heavier. This is because the strings must be thicker, heavier, and longer as the pitches become lower. In the winds, note the size of the tubas and the contrabassoons (see tuba, pp. 103–104).

With the string bass, the useable surface of the bow hair is 23 inches. The only way that 23 inches can be stretched to cover extra beats is to move the bow more slowly. Bow conservation is similar to wind conservation. The obvious difference is that the string player can *see* how much bow is available, but the wind player cannot see how much air is left. With the brasses, the moment the wind becomes too meager, the lips stop vibrating, and the tone vanishes. It is a nasty problem for them in long *diminuendos*.

There is a fundamental difference in the position of the bow as it rests on the string. The violin/viola technique tilts the bow away from the bridge, playing on the outer edge of the hair surface. The cello/bass tilts the bow toward the scroll or toward the player who plays on the inner edge of the hair. All of them use full hair surface most of the time.

These differences are caused by the fact that the cello and bass stand upright when played, whereas the violin and viola are parallel with the floor in playing position. The violin/viola bow approaches the four strings from the right-hand side of the highest pitched string; cello and bass approach their strings from the side of the lowest string. This fact reverses certain technical principles between the treble clef strings and those written for the bass clef.

All strings read the down-bow and up-bow indications identically. But there are times when the demands made by a series of fast, unslurred string crossings on a pair of neighboring strings necessitates opposing directions in the bow strokes of the various instruments.

EXAMPLE 21. For use in fast, unslurred string crossings

The reason for this accommodation also has to do with the natural direction of the motion of the hand in the wrist joint.

Violin/viola: A down-bow on the lower string and an up-bow on the higher string (unslurred bowing) permit unlimited speed in crossing the two strings.

On the **cello** and **bass**: long passages of fast, unslurred string crossings on neighboring strings require a down-bow on the upper string for infinite speed. In all four of the instruments, the motion of the hand is actually a very small clockwise circle.

When the music requires speed but arrives on the first of the crossing notes with the bow moving in the uncomfortable direction, the solution is to slur the first two notes and the last two notes of the passage to adjust the bowing for normal, customary usage as the music continues.

In summary, for a series of fast string crossings, unslurred, on neighboring strings, violinists and violists down-bow on the lower string. For a series of fast string crossings, unslurred, on neighboring strings, down-bow on the upper string of the cello or bass.

The change of direction of the bow stroke, from down to up and from up to down, is one of the refined string player's techniques. There is an everlasting tendency to rush into the change, simply because the bow is already moving rapidly and smoothly. A canny observation of Mademoiselle Nadia Boulanger in her classes at the Paris Conservatory was that pianists and violinists "always cheat the last note of a slurred passage. They precipitate the change to the following note."

This is a matter of ear-training, to hear the difference. To cure this performance mistake, practice purposely *holding out* the last note of the slurred phrase much longer than the rhythm demands. This trains poise into the pianist's fingers and into the bow at the end of its slurred stroke on the stringed instruments.

When the passage is eventually played in rhythm, the difference *is* noticeable, especially in the feeling of the continuous legato line.

For the thick cello C string and the much thicker bass strings, the added heft built into the bow itself is not enough to produce a fine big tone. These players learn to play "into the string"—to move a little more slowly with the bow and to keep its contact securely focused on the string.

Having the string player's left hand in the highest position, thereby shortening the distance between finger and bridge, helps with the tone and speeds the bow stroke.

CHAPTER FIVE

Practicing Sequences, Scales, and Accentuations (Substitution Accents)

As the motifs are used, they gradually (almost without the knowledge of the performer) build up speed. The time comes when new challenges are needed. These take two forms: using the motifs in sequence and eliminating the long note in the motif and replacing it with an accent.

When dealing with *sequence*, the mind cannot relax for even a moment, or mistakes will immediately begin to occur. Sequences move at a slightly slower rate than do the replacements by accents.

Using the accent for variety requires fast responses from the fingers and the mechanisms that produce the sound itself: the breath, its reaction on the lips or the reeds, and the bow's reaction on the strings.

The speed will be faster when using the accents and slower when using the motifs sequentially. Scales are ideal for applying these variations because the notes are sequential; the ear does not have to deal with new note arrangements.

Scales are most effective when the repetitious pattern completes itself as the scale arrives at the beginning again and starts over. For this reason, certain accommodations are introduced in Examples 23 and 24 for the two-octave and three-octave scales.

EXAMPLE 22. From Rondo, op. 20, no. 1, by Friedrich Kuhlau

As written
(A)

Sequence, four-note motifs from Example 16, A and B
(a)   (b)   (B)

Replacement accents
(a)   (b)   (C)

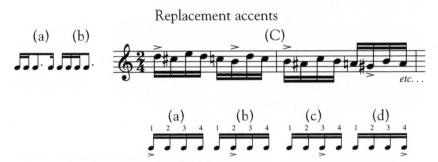

As for fingerings, the easiest are those of the strings. The fingers fall sequentially as the hand slides into the required positions. The brasses overblow by the octave, so the fingering repeats for the upper octaves. But the clarinetist overblows a twelfth and, therefore, has to readjust the fingerings for the second octave. The other woodwinds are similar to the brasses or the strings. The pianist has a dichotomy: it is easier for two hands to play the scale in contrary motion because the thumbs change position in both hands at the same moment and in the same manner as in parallel motion. When the scale is written in parallel octaves the thumbs move at different times, and the problem is more demanding.

EXAMPLE 23. Two-octave scale accommodations

For triplet renditions: no change. Begin and end on the key note. Repeat the top note to start the return direction for a total of fifteen notes. This pattern can accommodate three- and five-note groupings.

For rhythms in fours: Add an extra note at the end of the one-octave scale, and repeat that note to start the descending scale. The sixteen total notes can be used for groupings of two, four, or eight notes.

For groupings of two, three, six, or nine notes, two extra notes must be added at each end of the two-octave scale for a total of eighteen notes. The highest note does not repeat, but it starts the descending scale.

The three forms given in Example 23 set up practice patterns for note groupings in two, three, four, five, six, eight, or nine notes (slurred or accented). These passages can be accented in slurred or unslurred groups, or they can retain the accents in long slurs covering the entire length of the scale.

Don't overlook the fact that the accents can also be used sequentially as shown previously in Example 22. Speaking of sequence: let us look for a moment at the sequential use of the threes. They apply nicely to Example 23A.

EXAMPLE 24. Sequential uses of three-note groupings

(A)

(B)

(C)

(D)

(E)

By this time you may feel a bit intimidated by the sudden realization that there are myriad choices (and still more on the way). Relax! You do not have to use them all. But you do have to make a choice as to which way you will practice each etude or the troublesome passage. Here is a stepwise analysis for making the choice:

1. As always, get the sequence of the notes correctly in mind by playing the passage several times slowly, note by note.
2. Play it fast enough that you will miss the notes that have been bothering you.
3. Most important: *Notice which note and which finger started the trouble.*
4. Choose a pattern in which that finger lands on a long note.

Because the long note in the patterns always follows on the heels of the fast notes, the faulty finger will come down fast on the missed notes. The hand acquires its own feel for the correct note, and the sudden snapping down on the right note is made with great and sudden decision. Eventually, as the habits form, one begins to think that the fingers have little brains of their own. When the wrong finger tries to come down, the correct finger somehow gets there first, and the mistake does not happen.

When several fingers are involved, use each variation of the chosen practice pattern, and the other guilty fingers will find themselves arriving, in turn, on the long note.

No book on practicing can be complete without reference to the advanced techniques initiated by Ivan Galamian as described in his *Principles of Violin Playing and Teaching.*

First, Galamian added four notes to the three-octave scale, making a total of twenty-four notes: twenty-four is a magical number because it can be evenly divided into two, three, four, six, eight, and twelve notes per beat. These groupings can be slurred or unslurred, with or without obvious accents. With each reiteration of the scale, the next of the given number of notes per beat is added (starting with two and progressing up to twelve). This exercise gradually builds speed as more and more notes are crammed into the beat.

Second, this next manner of execution can be used to build breath control or bow control by starting with a slightly faster beat for the first time the scale is played and then adding beats to each note: two beats per note, three beats per note, and so on up to twelve beats per note.

The speed of the beat remains a constant throughout while the breath and the bow gradually move more slowly as additional beats are added to the notes. The sustaining power of the airflow and the bow-flow is gradually extended. Galamian, however, does not leave it here. He goes a few steps further.

EXAMPLE 25. The three-octave scale, twenty-four-note form

Wind, string, and piano players will be challenged by all of the following recommendations from Galamian. For the two-octave scales, see Example 23, p. 49 (Note: We will add some groupings for two-octave scales following the quoted three-octave material.) Here are some examples of Galamian's practice suggestions.

EXAMPLE 26. Practice suggestions for the two-octave scale

Slurred	Unslurred
[2 – 4 – 6]	[2 – 4 – 6]
2 + 6 + 4	2 + 6 + 4
4 + 2 + 6	4 + 2 + 6
4 + 6 + 2	4 + 6 + 2
6 + 2 + 4	6 + 2 + 4
6 + 4 + 2	6 + 4 + 2
1 + 3 + 8	1 + 3 + 8
1 + 8 + 3	1 + 8 + 3
3 + 1 + 8	3 + 1 + 8
3 + 8 + 1	3 + 8 + 1
8 + 1 + 3	8 + 1 + 3
8 + 3 + 1	8 + 3 + 1

EXAMPLE 27. Suggested slurrings for two-octave scales on p. 49 to be used slurred and unslurred.

(A) Fifteen-note form	(B) Sixteen-note form	(C) Eighteen-note form
2 + 3	2 + 6 + 8	2 + 3 + 4
3 + 2	2 + 8 + 6	2 + 4 + 3
4 + 1	4 + 3 + 1	4 + 2 + 3
1 + 4	4 + 1 + 3	4 + 3 + 2
1 + 3 + 1	3 + 4 + 1	3 + 1 + 5
2 + 1 + 2	3 + 1 + 4	3 + 5 + 1
		6 + 2 + 1
		6 + 1 + 2

There is enough material here to keep one busy for a long, long time. You don't have to play through all of the patterns, but the more ways you can play the scale, the more your general technique will improve (as well as your sight-reading). This is even more beneficial when using the arpeggio form.

Choose a different pattern every day in addition to your usual scale routine. Once a pattern is conquered, it loses its power to force you to concentrate. Also, new approaches add interest to the daily practice activities.

Chapter Six

Practicing Modern Innovations:
The Missing Technique

Modern composers have given us new problems to conquer *rhythmically* (the addition or deletion of an extra beat or part of a beat within the measure), *harmonically* (the glorification of discord), and *sequentially* (the moving of a few notes or measures of a melody line by changing its position in space—an octave or interval, higher or lower—thus breaking its sequential logic).

Because note sequence does not depend upon the rhythm, we are free to handle it in any way we wish as long as we do not alter the sequence itself. For example, the sequence is destroyed if any single note is doubled without doubling all of the notes.

Let us talk first about the rhythm. Among the often-encountered problems is the sudden insertion of a fifth unit among a series of fours (4/4, 5/4, 4/4) or the deletion or extension of a part of a rhythmic beat (4/4, 7/8, 4/4; 2/4 [4/8] to 5/8).

Rhythm: Checking the definitions of *rhythm* in several languages, the idea of "repetition" or "recurrence" is basic to them all. A motif by itself is not a rhythm until it is repeated at least once.

When composers interrupt a repetition by inserting a disconcerting unit into it, the music is no longer rhythmic. This means then that we are forced to deal not with a rhythm but with the individual units that make up the metric structure of the measure. We have to subdivide the rhythms and sort them out individually into some kind of logical pattern. Subdivision of note values helps with the solution.

EXAMPLE 28. Using note subdivisions

As printed:

Solution:

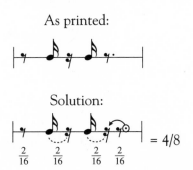

Mentally move dot to join the preceding sixteenth note

Standing by itself, the passage does not establish a rhythm; but when it is repeated as written there is a recurring rhythmic unit: the sixteenth note. Without the time signature, we are not quite sure what is going on. The problem here is one of notation. The final dotted eighth rest is confusing because we cannot immediately tell from the notation where the last beat begins.

Upon further analysis, the dot after the last rest signifies a sixteenth rest. When the sixteenth rest is placed in its true position (after the second sixteenth note), everything becomes instantly clear—it is a 2/4 (4/8) measure.

Here is a problem in accentuation. *This is one continuous exercise.*

EXAMPLE 29. Exercise in marked accents

Practice by repeating this in sequence while counting out the seven eighth notes in each measure until the *feeling* for the rhythm is established with the marked accents.

Harmony: To conquer today's "glorification of discord," the player has to take time to develop his or her consciousness of the intervals in fourths and major sevenths. So many modern etudes are written as though the pertinent technique had already been conquered. They do not take the player through the process of building the things not covered in the centuries-old fundamental techniques we customarily practice. To remedy this, try Example 30.

EXAMPLE 30. Technique for modern music

Reiteration of fourths:

Reiteration of major sevenths:

Get the intervals securely into the ear. Then choose from among the practice motifs to continue to build the speed. Finally, link the fourths into the broken-chord sequence of the two-octave or three-octave scale: C–F–B–E–A–D–G–C, applying the usually practice rhythms.

For the major sevenths, try Example 31.

EXAMPLE 31. Exercise in major sevenths

When you can play all of the above examples, use the intervals in one of the "modern rhythms," such as the one given in Example 29 (see also Example 32).

EXAMPLE 32. Sequences (other accentuations)—all even length

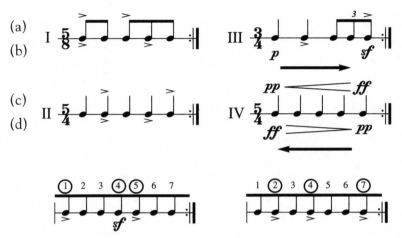

Start with the "lowest common denominator," the shortest written unit, and set the metronome to make the multiple beats for you. Think 1–2–3–4–5–6–7, and insert the accents on the numbers so indicated.

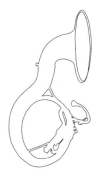

CHAPTER SEVEN

Practicing the Etudes:
The Lengthened Attention Span

Etudes follow rather standard patterns regardless of the instruments for which they are written. Either they emphasize a particular technique throughout, or they deal with difficult fingerings and slurrings inserted unexpectedly to upset the performance. Certain etudes are comprised of continuous sixteenth notes grouped in fours or threes that are scalewise in form, while others have many intervallic skips with a somewhat uniform type of intermittent slurring throughout.

The continuous etudes, slurred or unslurred, are usually designed to increase the speed of note reiteration. They often contain difficult harmonic sequences, and they may be slurred by measure to increase breath control or bowing steadiness and speed.

Intervallic etudes usually add various types of patterned slurrings mixed with passages of separately tongued or bowed notes. Some lean toward the arpeggio form throughout. It is amazing, looking through book after book, how absolutely universal sixteenth notes grouped in fours are.

Books for piano and strings add etudes in chords and double-stops, but they too can be classified under one of the headings given above.

Rodolphe Kreutzer's famous *Forty-two Etudes* for the violin has been transcribed for various wind instruments as well as for the lower strings, viola, and some for cello. Kreutzer builds individual techniques etude by etude. The studies by Pierre Gaviniès (also for violin) are almost entirely of the intervallic variety except three etudes in double-stops (numbers 1, 15, and 24).

For the piano, Czerny's op. 740, *The Art of Finger Dexterity*, has etudes of the continuous-runs variety throughout, which emphasize one hand or the other or both together.

Books of caprices go beyond pure etude form and show more variety and rhythmic change. They concentrate on the musical aspect rather than the purely technical.

The great majority of etudes written for piano and strings belong to the ages. Many of the finest etude books for these instruments were written between 1700 and 1900. The best etude books have proved their quality and effectiveness and have never been permitted to die out.

The overall result of practicing etudes is increased attention span and physical endurance. The modern approach to practicing etudes has gone through a change. Instead of just "learning the etude," the practice has now become a vehicle for improving overall techniques while studying the etude itself. The practice methods used can benefit the musician's entire technique even though only one etude is being learned.

It is important to decide which motifs can be effectively applied. For example, the continuous etude lends itself to all types of slurring patterns or accentuations as well as to changes in note groupings. An etude in fours can be practiced in threes. Through this process, the attention becomes intensely focused, and mistakes happen the minute the attention slips.

Changing the accentuation creates a whole new etude. Further, a chosen series of slurring patterns can be used six lines at a time instead of playing the whole etude with only one pattern. This adds variety and builds flexibility.

When the teacher assigns several ways of practicing, it saves lesson time as the teacher checks on all of the practicing assignments by having the student change from one to the next as he or she progresses through the etude. Further, approaching the etude with the added variations guarantees that the etude will be better learned than if it were practiced using only the composer's idea.

It is important for the student to have a clear concept of the goal set by the particular etude. And the point should be made that every etude has a few measures that are more difficult and must be given special attention. These problematic measures are conquered by removing them from the context of the complete etude and applying rhythmic motifs. Remember to reinsert the troublesome measures, using some repetition with the preceding and following measures attached.

Whenever repetition is applied, there must be a clean break between repetitions. One must be able to pull out of the repetition cycle when the passage is reinserted into the music. It is easy to get on a repetitious merry-go-round that makes it difficult to add something different. Here are some pertinent suggestions:

- Try playing the etude *pianissimo* throughout. It is not easy, for you may find yourself back in the eternal *mezzo forte*. Listen to the sound you are producing.

- Try alternating *pianissimo* and *fortissimo* every two measures. This is excellent for orchestral players because this exercise improves sight-reading of dynamics in rehearsals.

- Become phrasally conscious. Build the phrase to its climax, and relax it gradually toward its ending or, in etudes, to its transition to the new problem.

- There is no legislation in existence that requires etudes to be played unmusically. Try to do something more than just play the notes.

- Certain etudes are written with reiterated notes. If they are two-note groups, practice double tonguing. In strings, such etudes are excellent for improving the *spiccato* bowing. For four-note groups, practice starting each four on the up-bow.

Playing each written note twice or three times and, later on, alternating twos and threes note by note, are also a good practice techniques when the note sequence is made up of notes of equal time.

Etudes in a slow tempo are rare; they stress tonal development, are more closely related to performance pieces, and provide an opportunity to deal with phrasing. The first pages in Gaviniès contain such an etude. The emphasis is on tone quality, developing it, listening for tonal colors, and using the imagination to build the musical concept.

There are a few general principles to observe in etude practice:

- Do not force yourself to complete the hour once you realize that your hands and mind are nearing exhaustion. STOP and rest. You will only practice mistakes when this fatigue exists.

- When practicing extension fingerings (strings=outside the position, piano=large, wide chords) do so a bit at a time. Straining the hands slows down your practice a week at a time. Practice such passages by inserting them among other things for a few minutes several times during the hour. It is an overall time-saver to pay attention to any strain on the hands. Do not force them to continue; the hands will strengthen of their own accord just through use, day by day.

- Lifting the fingers high after each note "to build strength" is one of the worst fallacies of all. Your hands do not need any more strength than they automatically acquire through daily practice. What they *do* need are *flexibility and speed*. Strength does not build either of these. Strength changes the form of the muscles and causes the loss of much flexibility. Speed is impossible for any length of time without flexibility. (Watch Olympic runners. Notice that the winners show relaxation between steps and strength only when pushing off to the next step after the foot has touched the ground. The instant of relaxation while the foot is in the air contributes to the endurance.)

- As for a practice routine on etudes: It pays to play through *slowly the first time*, paying attention to the note sequence, noticing where the tough spots are located, and choosing a tempo for the practice thereafter that will be effective in the more difficult passages without producing a myriad of great fumbles.

- Then, take out the difficult spots and "woodshed" them as mentioned previously.

Strings: Be canny in your practice of etudes loaded with string crossings. A sloppy crossing spoils the tone on both strings. Use the fermata-rest for some of the practice, stopping to make sure that the crossing is clean, not cluttered with extraneous noises. Every time you stop and do this you are building that super *control* needed in speed playing.

Chapter Eight

Practicing Sight-Reading:
Why You Can't Sight-Read Easily

Years ago there was a popular music magazine published by Theodore Presser Company entitled *The Etude*. It featured all things musical: great artists, conductors, pianists, vocalists, violinists. Each issue also contained a large section (ten or more pages) of piano solos suitable for teaching.

Guy Maier of the famous piano-duo team wrote regularly for *The Etude*. His pages were known as "The Teacher's Round Table." In addition to his own monthly article, he also added an "Answers to Questions" section. Reading his material, one often picked up precious hints of a technical nature that were immensely helpful.

One questioner asked about sight-reading. He wrote that he was a concert pianist performing as a soloist with symphony orchestras. He had a large repertoire of concertos and filled many successful engagements each year. *But he couldn't sight-read* and was desperate for advice.

Here is a *summary* of Maier's answer.

Your problem is that you do not have a system in your approach to sight-reading. The following suggestions may be helpful: Get a book of simple four-part song writing, or other not-too-difficult music. Read each beat *starting with the lowest note in the left hand and progressing upward to the highest note in the right hand*. Set the fingers on the keys as you read. When the fingers are correctly set, play the chord and sustain it with the pedal while you set the notes for the next chord. You should experience a gradual improvement in your reading using this approach.

(This method has been tested with students majoring in instruments other than piano who must pass a piano proficiency in order to obtain their degrees. It has been effective and of value to such students. As the eyes became accustomed to following the pattern, the necessary speed gradually arrived.)

The music reading process is startlingly different from the reading of words. A word sequence is a solid unity comprised of single words, each one having an accepted meaning. But in music each symbol, each note, represents two ideas that must be read simultaneously: the pitch to play, along with how long it lasts, and the rhythm.

The mind is, therefore, required to deal with two concepts at the same time and to do so instantly. Missing a note pitch-wise is a personal problem. But missing a beat in ensemble performance truly upsets the applecart. The rehearsal has to stop while the problem is rectified.

Efficient sight-reading depends, first and foremost, upon the ability to recognize immediately where each beat starts within the measure. The rhythm has to become automatic in order to free the eyes to deal with the notes. This way the brain can deal with the other problems and not waste time stumbling over the rhythm.

The first law of sight-reading is to get to the next beat on time, no matter what you are currently playing. There is a psychological wrench in forcing oneself to continue uninterrupted when the eye and ear have told you that you "made a mistake." As stated above, missing a note is a personal problem, but missing a beat is fatal.

So how do we practice sight-reading?

First, we acquire the ability to group all notes into units that total one beat. When we can see where each beat starts, then we have the first skill under control.

Next, we must learn to live with that recurring beat, regardless of what we have played. This is a tough step.

The following advice comes from Clarence Evans, principal violist of the Chicago Symphony for some fifteen years in the 1920s–1930s.

> Choose a book of etudes, ensemble music, or orchestral parts that is *just a bit easier than you could play well*. Set a moderate tempo, and proceed to read each beat as it comes. Do not stop for any wrong notes or misplayed rhythmic motifs. KEEP GOING. *Get to the next beat on time* no matter what you may have played! Once you have forced yourself to keep going, the time will come when you will *see the mistake before you play it*.

How right he was! What will ultimately happen is that you will have such absolute faith in the accuracy of the printed notes that you will play them correctly "at sight." You will stop predicting in your mind what you expect to hear, and you will play what is printed.

Which is more important—notes or rhythm? The answer is: neither. But what is true is that most fatal errors are made in the playing of rhythms.

The problems with rhythm go back to Guido d'Arezzo (ca. 991–1033). He chose to start with the whole note as his fundamental. Because a whole note is comprised of four quarter notes, we have been required to think in fractions ever since—as the names of our note values state.

Now, everyone knows it is more difficult to add fractions than to add whole numbers. So if we recognize the note that signifies one beat and we group all symbols to total one full beat, we more quickly recognize exactly where each beat begins. The chart on page 68 comes from my book *Orchestral Bowings and Routines*.

In using the chart, all words or phrases are spoken rhythmically, in tempo, and during a single beat. To illustrate, "four-on-one-beat" is spoken during that one beat. This way of visually grouping notes into units of one beat has been tested for years, and it always works.

Professionals find it helpful to be able to recognize where the beats start within the measure, and it is preferable that young players acquire this knowledge right from the beginning. Referring to the chart: Words in quotation marks are spoken during one beat, unless otherwise indicated. Beat subdivisions are ignored until the unity of the beat itself is well established in the player's mind as he or she sight-reads.

TIME-COUNTING CHART FOR THE BEGINNER

NOTE		TERMINOLOGY
♩	equals	"One"
𝅗𝅥	equals	"One-Two"
𝅗𝅥.	equals	"One-Two-Three"
𝅝	equals	"One-Two-Three-Four"
♫	equals	"Part-ners"
♪.♪	equals	"LONG-short" ("partners")
♬♬	equals	"FOUR-on-ONE-beat"
♬	equals	"THREE-per-beat"
♪. ♪	equals	"One, Two-and"
𝄽	equals	"Rest"
▬	equals	"Rest, rest"
▬	equals	"Rest, rest, rest, rest"
♪𝄾	equals	"PART-ners" - Play only on "part" ⎫ Here one of the
𝄾♪	equals	"Part-NER" - Play only on "ners" ⎭ "part-ners" is a silent "partner."

When applied to the slow tempi where the eighth-note gets one beat, the quarter becomes "One, Two" and the "partners" are two sixteenth notes.

In fast 6/8, note the relationship:

In 4/4	♩	equals	ONE;	equals	♩.	in 6/8.
In 4/4	𝅗𝅥	equals	ONE-TWO;	equals	𝅗𝅥.	in 6/8.
In 2/4	𝅗𝅥	equals	ONE;	equals	♬♬	in 6/8.

It is seldom the finding of *what* note to play that trips the young musician in sight-reading. It is confusion as to *when* to play that makes him or her a poor sight-reader.

From Orchestral Bowings and Routines *by Elizabeth A. H. Green. Bryn Mawr, PA: American String Teachers Association* ©*1949: 86–87. Used with permission. One addition has been made to this chart: the triplet figure is identified by the words "three-per-beat," spoken during one beat.*

In item nine on the chart, the dotted quarter plus eighth: the dot extends the note, so *one* extends into *two*. *One* must wait until after *two* starts for the music to continue. The beat falls *on* the dot, which is *two*.

The basic unit in all math systems is *one*, so the note that corresponds to *one* is basic. In any time signature, let the note that gets one beat become the controlling factor.

When dealing with the "unity of the beat," we cannot be eternally fussing with fractions. For example, two eighth notes equal one beat in 2/4, 3/4, 4/4, etc., but mathematically two eighths can never equal the number 1. This substantiates the fact that our musical math is completely illogical. No wonder children have trouble with it. It just does not march to our rhythmic demands.

There is one more item that will be helpful. There are three things that are most often missed when young people sight-read: First comes the dotted quarter note. Second is a measure that begins with a quarter note followed by faster notes. Seeing the fast notes, the mind rushes to start them. Emphasize that no matter what follows the quarter note, it does not start until the *next* beat. The third thing that causes trouble is the half note. This is because students fail to hold it through the second beat.

The stringed instrument player has the further sight-reading problem of dealing with the bowing and the almost unlimited fingering possibilities of the violin and the viola. When sight-reading, one is not always lucky enough to instantly pick the one fingering that may solve a difficulty. In many cases some diligent study may be required before smoothness arrives.

There are other effective bits and pieces that can come into play momentarily during sight-reading. Sometimes the eyes unexpectedly recognize something else in the music that helps with the up-tempo sight-reading performance. These aids are:

- Quick recognition of a harmonic interval.

- Chromatic relationships.

- The name of the note—especially in reading double flats and double sharps.

- Violin and viola: In all odd-numbered positions (one, three, five, and seven) the notes on the lines are played by the odd-numbered fingers, one and three. This helps in fast string crossings with wide skips note-wise.

- Viola, cello, and string bass: Work on the instant recognition of clefs together with their fingering systems.

- Wind instruments: Work on the instant recognition of transposition intervals and their fingerings.

- Strings: Keep the eyes and ears alert for musical styles, e.g., legato, staccato. If the passage is staccato, which variety? *Martelé, spiccato*, etc.? There are six varieties of staccato bowing plus the separation between notes of the *louré* (slurred) articulation.

- For all instruments: When measures are repeated in identical notation, it is usually safe to let the eyes skip ahead to plan for the new material. The mind and hands can carry on without the eyes. But be sure to notice the number of measures.

Things That Momentarily Disturb the Reading

- A sudden encounter with double sharps and double flats.

- Unexpected note relationships; unprepared modulations.

- Passages of clumsy fingerings.

- Sudden clef or transposition changes.

- Difficult cross rhythms.

- Chromatic scales with a whole step inserted here or there.

- Long skips involving ledger lines.

- Strings: Poorly notated harmonics. (This can literally stop a rehearsal until the concertmaster looks at the score.)

A good sight-reader allows neither "hell nor high water" to impede him or her from arriving on the next beat on time. Life moves on in the fast lane, and traffic is less predictable when the driving power is sight-reading.

Chapter Nine

Practicing the Piano—A Stringed Instrument: Its Uniqueness

It is not customary to think of the piano as a stringed instrument, but all tone (formed by pressing the piano keys) comes from the tapping of the so-called "hammers" as they impinge upon the stiff metal strings under great tension.

This mechanism is an outright miracle. When the player pushes down any one key, dozens of moving parts within the piano are activated. It is not just that one hammer has been sent on its way, but that the head of that hammer has to recoil instantly after making its tap. Then the hammer waits to settle back into its usual groove until the player releases the key. Further, the vibration that has begun in the strings must be stopped before the next note is played. The dampers stop the tone as soon as the key is released. If this were not so, there would be no clarity in passages of fast runs.

The dampers rest against the strings, and their mechanical action is connected to the hammer action. When the key is pressed, the damper simultaneously releases the strings, allowing the note to sound. The damper waits until the player releases the key. Releasing the key permits the damper to resume its position against the strings, stopping the vibration. If it is desirable to have the sound continue, the player presses the sustaining pedal—the one on the right in the row of three pedals.

All of the above has to be refined until everything works as easily, instantly, and effectively as the player may wish.

There also has to be uniformity among the keys so that the performer is not disconcerted as he or she sails through the repertoire in performance.

Piano artistry: Artist-teachers of piano engage in producing tonal variety by stressing the manner in which the keys are depressed or struck. Many shades of tonal color result, especially with the addition of the sustaining pedal. When the pedal is depressed *before* the chord is played, the strings not struck by the hammers add their bit of resonance through the phenomenon known as *sympathetic vibration*.

To explain: Objects tuned to similar pitches, such as octaves or other intervals of the "chord of nature" (see Example 33) will begin to vibrate slightly when any of the related notes are set into vibration by another source. The sound waves travel through the air, or other medium, and impinge upon the related object, setting it into vibration also.

This type of vibration is a fact of nature. It has to do with resonance, and it is most active in the stringed instruments. Players of the bowed strings rely upon it for judging accuracy in the tuning process. It is not unusual for such a player, when standing next to a silent piano while practicing, to suddenly hear some note he or she just played audibly echoed by the piano strings.

The pianist uses this phenomenon to create color in the piano sound. A chord, struck before the sustaining pedal has been depressed, can produce the illusion of a slight *crescendo* by activating the pedal instantly after the chord is played. A bit of richness develops as the other strings respond by sympathetic vibrations.

When Russian pianist Boris Berezovsky substituted for one of the "greats" a few years ago, he played a concert that had the general audience hypnotized and transported the fine pianists in attendance to regions of delight seldom witnessed. All that any of them could talk about were the "many colors" they heard in the concert: at times a "gentleness that was like a barely perceptible fog on a dark day or a brilliance like the sun flashing through space."

The point of all of this is that the player must first have a concept in mind of the effect he or she wishes to produce and then spend thousands of hours building the technique to produce it. To train the ear to hear the slightest variance in the sound is a masterstroke of patience.

As we proceed, let us remember that "some pianos have 7,000 separate parts in the action, which means approximately 80 parts per key" (Rigden, 163). (Also highly recommended for readers desiring more information is *Exploring Music: The Science and Technology of Tones and Tunes* by Charles Taylor.)

We turn now to the words of a much-respected professional pianist and teacher. Estelle Titiev begins by calling attention to the shrugged shoulders that far too many children exhibit in the beginning stages. This should be noticed immediately and corrected, especially in the first lessons. Relaxed shoulders permit free motion in the arm as the hands move toward the extremities of the keyboard.

Tone or "touch" as it is called *can be taught*. On the piano, it starts from the surface of the key. The key should be pushed down, not struck. The closer the fingers stay to the keys, the faster they will be able to play as technique grows and becomes habitual. (This is true also of the other instruments mentioned in this book.)

The arms hang loosely from the shoulder, and the elbows are bent to form a right angle with the upper arm. Attention is paid to the height of the piano stool, which should enable the child's hands to reach the keyboard from a level position without having to slant upward. The wrists and hands are then in a level position and can move easily in the required direction, either away from center or back to it. The wrist tends to precede the motion of the hand itself, a motion that starts from the relaxed shoulder. The hand follows the arm and wrist.

"Touch" is a topic for endless discussion (and, in some cases, for argument). There are those who study the piano in the science laboratory who doubt that the pianist can change the touch enough to make a difference in the sound. But the way a player presses the keys *can* make a difference.

Hitting the keys from high in the air with physical strength produces a strident tone. Many high harmonics are mingled with the tone, and the beautiful resonance of the lower harmonics is partially overshadowed. Contrarily, moving a bit more slowly and pushing the keys down (leaning into them instead of hitting them) does give more depth to the resultant sound. The hammer strikes less suddenly and less forcefully. The lower stroke gives precedence to the lower overtones.

Feeling depth of sound, *imagining* depth of sound, *listening* for resonance—all of these are concepts that add effectiveness to the performance. Teaching the ear to listen and to hear is fundamental to effective performance.

An artist gets the hands under control before they strike the keys again. It is not necessary to break the hammers in order to activate the brilliant high overtones. Excitement builds as a *crescendo* progresses, but chord quality involves technique, not just emotion.

The art of pedaling: The strings are set into the piano thus:

- From G below middle C, all the way to the treble end of the keyboard, the strings are grouped into sets of three for each pitch. The hammer hits all three simultaneously to produce the sound.

- From the above-mentioned G down one octave, the strings are grouped in twos. And from the F below this second octave, there is only one very thick (wound) string for each note.

- The three pedals do three different things: The one on the right keeps the dampers from springing back to stop the vibration. The one on the far left moves the entire row of hammers forward about an inch, giving them less space to travel before they contact the strings. This produces a softer tone. The pedal in the middle is the "tricky" one. It lifts the last row of dampers off the strings (from the E below middle C to the bass end of the keyboard). When playing a staccato chord in the range above middle C with the middle pedal depressed, one hears a faint, far-off echo of the chord.

Here are some experiments to try, playing around with sympathetic vibration. Do not use any pedals.

Experiment 1: Push down middle C silently, and hold it down while you play a staccato note on the C below. The struck note is dampened immediately, but you will hear the middle C very clearly while you hold down the key.

Experiment 2: Try this octave by octave, going upward (Example 33).

EXAMPLE 33. Right-hand plays silent notes, left-hand staccato

Experiment 3: With the right hand, silently hold down the chord middle C–E–G. Strike (staccato) the same chord an octave lower in the left hand. The "silent" chord has now been activated. Be sure that all three fingers of the left hand have struck the keys with equal force. If the third finger hits harder, you may hear the corresponding E louder in the "silent" chord. As the E fades out, the G may emerge. The harmonics (overtones) decay at different rates of speed.

EXAMPLE 34. Set chord silently

Experiment 4: Use the same chords an octave higher. The E and G may be louder than the C in the silent chord. It makes a difference whether the pedal is activated before the chord is played or after it has sounded. We have already mentioned the illusion of *crescendo* when the sustaining pedal is activated immediately after a chord has been played.

A change of chord implies the use of the pedal—probably releasing and resetting it instantly. Tone color can be changed by a combination of pedals.

The pedal on the right is not just used to make the sound louder or to carry it over to the next measure or section. Use of a "flutter" pedaling can add to the effects available.

The pedal is the palette of the artist.

(Note: In the manufacturing of the piano, adjustments have been made in the natural overtone series. The upper overtones are out of tune. Also, the half-step intervals are slightly off, mathematically. But these "discrepancies" are what give the piano its own tonal quality. If the instrument is badly out of tune, do not expect perfect results from the sympathetic vibration experiments.)

CHAPTER TEN

Practicing Double-Stops and Chords:
For the Bowed Strings

There is no better way to refine intonation than to practice double-stops and chords—which are unplayable for the winds. Small inaccuracies in intonation become more obvious when note sounds against note.

For the bowed strings and the piano, the performance of two notes simultaneously becomes part of everyday life. Because the pianist can do virtually nothing regarding intonation, the strings exercise authority over the double-stop technique.

Fundamentally, it is easier to bow on two strings than on just one. It takes less careful control. Students should be alerted to the several "bow levels" for the arm when bowing on one string at a time (Diagram 1).

DIAGRAM 1. Bow levels on one string

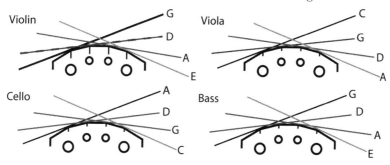

This is where the violin and viola part company with the cello and bass. The highest pitched strings are nearest the bow arm on the smaller instruments and farthest from the bow arm on cello and bass. Bow levels are, therefore, reversed. To bow on two strings, one simply moves halfway between the two bow levels of the pair of strings being used. The angle between the two levels is bisected.

To begin to build double-stop technique, one of the notes is fingered, and the other is the next lower open string. The immediate challenge is to become accustomed to bowing on two strings at once (Example 35). Bow each double-stop four times.

EXAMPLE 35. Building double-stop technique

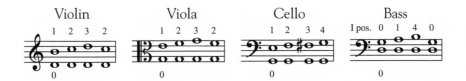

Once the bow is secure, the next step is to introduce sixths. Sixths fall on neighboring strings using neighboring fingers. The cellist has to choose which finger to use because the second and third fingers play half steps.

EXAMPLE 36. Introducing sixths

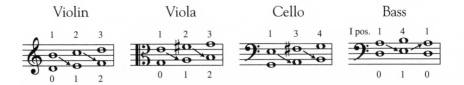

The third step is to build up to the octave. This sets the frame of the hand (a Galamian expression). From first finger on the lower string to fourth finger on the upper string (violin, viola), the hand spans an octave in all seven positions as it moves up the neck of the instrument.

EXAMPLE 37. Building up to the octave

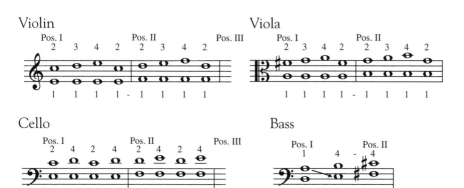

Danger: Do not practice for long periods of time when the little finger has to reach. If the hand tires, STOP! Practice something else for a while and come back to the octave study. Straining the hand slows everything down a week at a time.

The lower note of the octave is the control note. Train the ear to listen to it. Because the ear hears the highest pitch most quickly, it often neglects to listen to the lower note. Set the lower note in tune, then make all adjustments with the fourth finger. Too often the students fuss around with both fingers and waste time with no positive result.

When playing octaves on the cello, the thumb has to replace the first finger as the lower note of the octave. The span is too great for the hand.

Scalar passages in thirds, sixths, and octaves are written for the bowed strings and the piano. Double-stops on the piano may be played by one hand alone or by two hands in parallel motion. When the players have solved these problems, again apply the rhythms.

Practicing: When double-stops come sequentially in rapid passages, there are times when the two fingers do not arrive simultaneously on the strings. This happens when both fingers have to cross strings at the same time. In this case, choose a rhythm where the faulty fingers follow a fast note (e.g., after a sixteenth in the dotted-eighth sixteenth pattern). The necessity to move instantly into position helps the synchronization.

EXAMPLE 38. Double-stop practice

Chords: It may be unnecessary to mention that chords come in three-note and four-note forms. However, the bowing technique is different for the two types of chords.

To attack the three-note chord, the bow aims for the middle string of the three, depressing it sufficiently to pick up the two strings on either side. The closer the bow is to the bridge, the more difficult (or even impossible) it is to sound the three strings simultaneously. Moving too far away from the bridge produces a weak sound, and with applied pressure a scratch tone results. Adding speed to the bow after the attack can help in many instances.

The four-note chord starts on the two lower strings and finishes on the two upper strings. It can also be produced as a one plus three. The down-bow is preferred, especially if the chord stands alone.

Starting at the frog of the bow, softly and with *very little bow*, make the crossing to the upper strings suddenly and with power. This crossing takes place before two inches of bow have been used. The suddenness, with its equally sudden application of power, seems to "kick" the lower strings as the bow leaves them. The sound of the big four-note chord arrives.

Children fear the crossing. They tend to use almost half of the bow before they try to reach the upper strings. This defeats the purpose. I have a policy of *not* touching children in lessons, but it saves hours of frustration if this policy is set aside when teaching the four-note chord.

After the youngster has the chord "all set," take his or her bow hand, and give a warning not to drop the instrument when the sudden crossing is made. Once the child has *felt* the tiny amount of bow at the beginning and the full, brilliant, confident stroke that follows, the idea is grasped very quickly. It is just a "fun" moment in the lesson. You will probably never have to do this more than once.

For the one-plus-three rendition, aim for the middle string when crossing. (These paragraphs apply to the brilliant, *forte*, down-bow chords.)

For a legato rendition, the crossing can be made more slowly and have an organ-like quality that binds the notes together. Usually such renditions are applicable when the chord is part of the melodic sequence. Consecutive passages of such chords are bowed down, up, down, and so on.

Chords for the strings must be arranged note-wise so that each note is on a different string and written at an interval that can be spanned by the fingers. Sometimes in a chord one finger will cover two strings with the notes being a perfect fifth apart.

EXAMPLE 39. Practicing chords

(A)

Fingering:

(B)

Violin   Viola

etc...

Practicing: For practicing, group the chords in twos, threes, or fours. Use the long-short and short-long rhythms as well as the motifs grouped in threes. Apply the fermata-rest as needed.

---

* Recommended for student use introducing double-stops: *Melodious Double-Stops Book 1 and 2* by Josephine Trott (Schirmer Books). This is an excellent resource because for the first eight exercises one note is an open string.

PART TWO:
The Instruments as the Professionals See Them

Chapter Eleven

The Woodwinds: Flute, Oboe, Clarinet, Saxophone, Bassoon

This chapter is devoted to woodwind instruments. The strings will have their shining moments in the coming chapters when we deal with the many techniques that are theirs alone.

The flute: Chinese scholar Mei-Po Chao wrote a small but priceless volume he entitled *The Yellow Bell*. In it he told of a countryman who, emerging from the mists of the ages, cut a piece of reed and blew the first note of music, "the yellow bell"—a note that gradually produced the five-tone scale and a simple reed that eventually became the silver (or even golden) flute of today.

By cutting reeds of given lengths, the five tones of the Chinese scale materialized.* They arrived in this order: the fundamental, the fifth, the supertonic, the sixth, and the mediant. *Do, sol, re, la, mi.* The interval of the fourth was missing! Thus far everything was perfect. But to cut a reed of more than one length for an added tone, our researcher encountered mathematical fractions. Therefore, only the five tones were considered worthy of acceptance as absolute perfection.

The flute is unique in the wind family because it has no round mouthpiece like the brasses and no reed like other woodwinds. It has only an open hole to blow across. The stream of air impinges on the metal just below the far side of the open hole while the player's lips are responsible for tone quality, pitch, and volume.

Glennis Stout, expert teacher and sought-after lecturer on flute, says, "The slit between the lips through which the air column flows is not round. It is longitudinal, narrow in height and small in lengthwise extension. The size can be adjusted by the performer to correct pitch variations. The instrument is held so that the top surface is level horizontally, or nearly so.

"Work on the headjoint alone should be the first order of business for a beginning flute student. Feeling at ease with the position of the flute on the lower lip (which must cover one-third of the hole when the student is blowing) and being able to blow a steady stream of air—not just hard puffs—are crucial to the development of a good tone. The lips should never be tight or drawn back at the corners. Relaxed lips are essential to the development of a good embouchure, which will result in a beautiful tone. (And this is possible, even for beginners.)

"Have students think 'pooh' when they start the airstream, and when they can control the airstream, they can learn to start the tone with their tongues, saying a gentle 'too.'

"Beginners on the flute spend their initial days practicing just on the headjoint. The trick of blowing across the center of the hole is where everything begins. Using just the headjoint, the pitch can be made to drop an octave by covering the opening at the end with the palm of the hand."

Leone Buyse is professor of flute and chamber music at Rice University, a former principal flutist of the Boston Symphony and the Boston Pops Orchestra, and an exquisite soloist. She mentions the high, middle-octave C-sharp on the flute, a bane to all players. To correct it, "Angle the airstream lower by relaxing the lower lip and pulling the upper lip down a bit. Dropping the lower jaw slightly is also helpful. Sharp notes in the top octave can often be helped by adding a key or (on an open-holed flute) the rim of a key."

Both of our experts mention the need for an open throat and the use of vowel sounds (see similarities with French horn, pp. 97–99 and tuba, pp. 103–104).

To facilitate holding the flute while playing, Buyse mentions an idea that may be useful for teachers of beginners. She suggests the words "balancing the flute" instead of "holding the flute." She explains, "This is less likely to produce the tense grip many beginners apply to the instrument.

"The base knuckle of the first finger of the left hand index finger pushes the instrument toward the player. The thumb of the right hand (under the F key) pushes the instrument slightly forward, away from the player. The instrument consequently has good contact with the chin just *below the lower lip*, and the player feels secure. All of this produces a feeling of 'balance' while supporting the instrument."

Buyse adds some interesting tips from famous twentieth-century flutists whom she has known:

In discussing articulation, Michel Debost (Oberlin Conservatory faculty, formerly principal flutist of l'Orchestre de Paris and professor at the Paris Conservatory) speaks of the consonant "t" as being essentially dental. During her studies with Debost, Buyse came to believe that Americans, who generally pronounce "t" more like "d," need to make a conscious effort to articulate further forward in the mouth. The resulting articulation will be crisper, and tone quality will be better focused.

Robert Dick, well-known avant-garde flutist and composer, uses the terminology "throat tuning." He suggests imagining the position one's throat would assume to sing a given pitch before playing it.

The late Marcel Moyse, esteemed French pedagogue and founding member of the Marlboro Colony, urged his students to develop a broad palette of tone colors by working on interpretation. He recommended listening to violinists and opera singers to develop a more imaginative sense of color on the flute.

Finally, Buyse reminds us, "Raising the flute too high on the lips tends to sharpen the overall pitch and to lessen the possibility of producing a warm, full, resonant sound. Always listen attentively while practicing, and when experimenting, notice when a physical change results in an audible improvement. Working toward instrumental mastery is invariably most successful when a player enjoys the journey."

Oboe: The oboe, a double-reed instrument, is conical in bore, closed at one end, and overblows the octave. The fingering is repetitive.

In describing his approach to the oboe, Harry Sargous, who served as solo oboist in the Toronto (Canada) Symphony Orchestra, speaks of the teaching of Robert Bloom, the famous oboist of the NBC Symphony during the years 1937–1943 at the outset of Toscanini's conductorship. Bloom was insistent upon the use of the metronome from the first days of the student's introduction to the oboe. Very slow tempos could be set, but the need to establish the feeling of the inevitable arrival of the next beat on time was of paramount importance with Bloom. (We should qualify this with the reminder that many students arrive at the "oboe stage" after having become actively acquainted with the clarinet.)

(Note: Experimental work with junior high orchestral students has shown that a few of the children had not established within themselves the feeling of the eternal reiteration of the beat—the fundamental of all orchestral performance. If asked to beat time for the group, there were always a few who wanted to beat articulations as well.)

Sargous emphasizes the sensitivity of the oboe's double reed and the need for the performer to pay attention to his or her embouchure before placing the reed between the lips. (A close parallel is found in Cooper's discussion of the bassoon, which is also a double-reed instrument, on pp. 93–95.)

To quote Sargous: "Care should be taken to prepare the embouchure—the mouth cavity, the sections of the tongue, the cheeks and lips—while placing the tip of the double reed between the lips. Precision here pays dividends in musical results." (Here Sargous suggests a cross-reference to the words of Robert Dick and Marcel Moyse, p. 89.)

As for the fingering system of the oboe: "Whereas the clarinet has open holes to be covered by the fingers, the oboe has a myriad of keys to do the job. Legato is more difficult with the oboe. As a result, oboists often have seven fingers between notes. It requires careful coordination to overcome mechanical problems, which can easily foil the smooth legato."

Once again we find an outstanding teacher recommending the deletion of the word "attack" for the tongue and suggesting its replacement with the idea that the tongue acts as a valve to release the air, allowing it to flow through the instrument so that a more musical tone quality results.

The oboe occupies a very special place in the color palette of the orchestra. Its tone is so very clear that it penetrates the orchestral sound but never calls undesirable attention to itself. This makes it an ideal solo instrument, and the orchestral repertoire furnishes it with many beautiful opportunities. (Note that the oboe sets the standard when the professional orchestra tunes.)

One word about the overtones: In the oboe, the fundamental is often *nearly overshadowed* by the strength of several of the higher overtones, and this accounts for its special tone quality.

The clarinet: The solo qualities of the clarinet are well known in both the orchestra and the band. The clarinet contributes to band music much of what the violin sections do for the symphony.

Michael Webster, formerly principal clarinetist of the San Francisco Symphony and Rochester Philharmonic, says, "Unlike any other instrument, the clarinet produces alternate rather than consecutive harmonics so that the second register is an octave plus a fifth above the lower register. Filling in that gap creates a lot of extra work for the left thumb and index finger as well as both pinkies. Connecting registers smoothly between B-flat (third line, treble clef) and B-natural (the infamous 'break') poses a unique technical challenge for clarinetists."

EXAMPLE 40. A passage for second clarinet from *Daphnis et Chloe*, Part 3, by Maurice Ravel. The figure is repeated four times consecutively in the same measure.

For ease, the right-hand fingers very often can be set *before* crossing when they will not affect the pitch after the crossing.

Lengthy passages of fast sequential staccato tonguings are tiring. When unbearable, the subtle addition of a single two-note slur on unaccented notes can help.

For the E-flat soprano clarinet and the alto and bass clarinets, the fingering system remains the same. However, some adjustments have to be made in correcting pitches. Crossing the break is similar, except that with the bass clarinet it is a bit more difficult.

The alto clarinet for the band is in E-flat. For orchestral use there is an alto clarinet in F called the bassethorn. The bass clarinet is in B-flat and is used in both band and orchestra. (Note: The letter name attached to the name of the instrument tells its transposition interval, relative to the note C, and the composer transcribes the parts as he or she writes them. For the clarinet in B-flat, the part is notated one whole tone higher than it is to sound. Instruments that do not transpose are called C instruments, in which a written C sounds a C.)

B-flat clarinet players will do well to become facile in transposing parts written for the A clarinet against the time they do not have an A instrument at hand.

One beautiful advantage the clarinet has over all brass instruments is the ability to hold out a *diminuendo* until it disappears into silence. In this facet, it joins the strings. (With brasses, the minute the wind becomes too weak, the lips simply stop vibrating and the tone is gone.)

The saxophone: The youngest member of the traditional woodwind family is the saxophone, patented by Adolphe Sax in Paris in 1846. Sax took advantage of the many improvements and discoveries that had been applied to the other instruments as they developed.

The saxophone is a single-reed instrument that overblows the octave and has no difficult break to cross. The scale goes straight through its range.

Donald Sinta (the saxophonist who is preferred by many of the fine professional orchestras today) says, "The fingering system is so easy it may almost be approached carelessly. The fingering of a one-octave scale repeats in the other octaves, and many keys have been added to facilitate speed and intonation."

The particular color of the saxophone tone is refined by the performer's skill for symphonic playing. As a jazz instrument, the saxophone is *par excellence*, carrying the melody much of the time and contributing to the improvisation. Its facile fingering system makes it ideal for improvisation.

There are two prestigious works for saxophone with orchestral accompaniment: the Concerto by Alexander Glazunov (1934) and the Concertino da Camera by Jaques Ibert (1935) for saxophone and chamber orchestra. Both were performed many times by the Danish saxophonist Sigurd Rasher during his international concert tours. Contemporary concertos have been written by Karel Husa and Ingolf Dahl.

The saxophone family includes soprano in B-flat, alto in E-flat, tenor in B-flat, baritone in E-flat, and the bass saxophone in B-flat. As with other low bass instruments, the bass saxophone requires more wind from the player (see tuba, pp. 103–104).

The bassoon: In general, the bassoon furnishes the bass line for the entire woodwind family, descending to B-flat just below the bass clef staff. (For reference, it is one whole tone lower than the lowest note on the cello.) As with the oboe, the bassoon is a double reed, conical bore instrument that overblows to the octave.

It has been said of our quoted expert, L. Hugh Cooper (a member of the Detroit Symphony for many years and professor of music at the University of Michigan since 1945), that he "knows more about the bassoon than any other six members of the human race."

Cooper speaks of the octave from low F below the bass staff up to the fourth line F as the "primary" register of the bassoon. From this fourth-line "open" F there are three additional sets of harmonic fingerings derived from the primary register that extend the bassoon's orchestral range up to high F-natural, treble clef top line.

"The bassoon offers an almost infinite number of alternate fingering possibilities," Cooper says. He wrote an encyclopedic type book, *Essentials of Bassoon Technique,* which contains several hundred fingerings presented in context with their musical applications.

In common with other experts mentioned, Cooper stresses the introduction of alternate fingerings early in the student's study of the instrument. "It is especially important with beginners and intermediate students so as to avoid developing premature habitual finger patterns. Make sure that the students learn to think and to 'wiggle' their fingers mechanically.

"The most important lesson of all is the very first one, while those that follow diminish in relative importance. A beginning student fortunate enough to have a great teacher doesn't need one later on.

"Don't let students play a note until confident that the correct sequential procedures are understood." (The reader will find Cooper's teaching outline of the "sequential procedures" in Chapter 16, p. 128.)

As an interesting sidelight, Cooper spoke of Simon Kovar, "teacher of many of the outstanding bassoonists of his generation."

According to Cooper, Kovar used a methodical yet cerebral approach for developing technical proficiency called "picking fingers." This involved having all digits on both hands in position slightly above their keys and finger holes, and then conceptualizing the complete finger pattern of a desired note. When sure, the player snaps the *complete* finger pattern down on the instrument with audible force at the command of "set!" Without playing the note, the player mentally checks for accuracy. If all proves to be correct, then, and only then, should the player produce the note. He or she continues the "picking" process throughout the passage, expanding the time frame between notes as necessary to avoid making any errors. (Note: It would seem that the fermata-rest came into being long before this book was begun.)

Cooper continues, "Practicing on the advanced level should use varied fingerings, mastering all of the possibilities, then choosing those that are most effective musically. Alternate the fingerings. Be able to produce the correct note in more than one way.

"Often the mechanical difficulties encountered in florid technical passages may be traced directly back to lack of basic control involving a single finger. For example, the left ring finger is notably erratic for right-handed performers (C–D–C), while the right ring finger proves difficult to lift and reset rapidly for left-handed players (G–A–G). In any respect, these and/or other errant digits must be identified and then disciplined through specific systematic practice until equal finger dexterity is achieved.

"The teacher of advanced students finds it necessary to spend too much time correcting faults that should have been taken care of years before they had become habitual. It is difficult to change a thoroughly rehearsed habit.

"One of the crucial errors is lifting the fingers off high above the keys and/or finger holes. The student then struggles to acquire the necessary speed for his advanced playing. Keep the fingers close, even *on* the keys between the notes. Time cannot be wasted getting the fingers into position to play."

Nothing has been said thus far about the bassoon's so-called "whisper" or "*pianissimo*" key. It is "normally activated by the left thumb and/or the left little finger. In spite of its misleading nomenclature, this key is really the bassoon's second-register key, which alternately closes or opens the small (.9 mm), rather ineffective second-register vent hole located in the bassoon bocal. (The bocal is a small metal tube that connects the attached reed to the instrument itself.)

The important thing to remember about this key is that its mechanical linkage functions just the *opposite* of all other woodwind register keys including the contrabassoon. The player must press the key to close the register vent and to remain in the primary octave. Releasing the key opens the vent and expedites shifting to the upper modes.

The contrabassoon's tube length and bore diameter are approximately twice those of the bassoon. It sounds an octave below the bassoon itself.

---

* *The Yellow Bell* was mentioned in the Library of Congress records as dating from 1907. The copy to which I refer is a "private publication" dated 1934, the same year I discovered it. The little legend was originally expanded to eight tones, including half steps. It was thoroughly scientific and is an authentic explanation of Chinese music written by Mei-po Chao, who was Instructor of Music, University of Shanghi and Lauéat de Conservatoire Royal de Musique de Bruxelles.

CHAPTER TWELVE

The Brasses: French Horn, Trumpet/Cornet, Trombone, Euphonium, Tuba

The brass instruments deal intimately with the natural overtone series. Building *upward* from the note C, the sequence is as follows: C (the fundamental), octave, fifth above; then C, E, G, B-flat (out of tune in the octave series, making it a problem for all wind instruments), C of the fourth octave, and proceeding on up in scale tones.

It is possible for the "chord of nature" (the overtone series as spelled out above) to form over any given pitch as a fundamental. The French horn in F forms the F series. The double horn adds the B-flat series. Notes not present in the harmonic series of the instrument are formed by the addition of three valves. The valves open longer sections of the instrument's tubing. As the tubing lengthens, the pitch goes down. Thus, the longer the instrument is, the lower the range of its pitches.

The notes of the harmonic series can be played without using the valves. They are called "open" tones. Adding this or that valve gives access to another overtone series. The performer changes from one to another of the open tones by the skill he or she develops in the lips.

French horn: Before the invention of the valve, the French horn was provided with a series of "slides"—portable lengths of tubing that could be inserted for playing in the various keys. The handicap was that when a modulation occurred in the music, the horn player had to be given time to insert the proper tubing. Prior to the use of slides, the horn was played in its "natural state" using the hand inside of the bell to adjust pitches.

Method books for the French horn begin, for the most part, with middle C followed by the ascending five scale tones. Louis J. Stout (associate principal hornist of the Chicago Symphony for a number of years and one of the world's most skillful teachers) calls attention to this fact. He adds: "They should also go down for the five notes below C. This would help to prevent the unfavorable attitude that often develops concerning the lower register of the horn. The student should develop both registers *equally* right from the beginning."

Stout comments on technique: "*The lips are the horn.* They are responsible for much of what is a formidable technique. To enumerate: In addition to the skills of the breath and the tongue, the horn player must be completely at home with the thirteen transpositions. He or she must be able to read them at sight when they suddenly occur in the music. Further, the player must also be ready with two ways to read the bass clef (according to the period and the country in which the music was written). He or she is responsible for certain lip trills and for the techniques of double tonguing, triple tonguing, and hand stopping.

"To correct an out-of-tune note, the player can adjust it by lipping, by using an alternate fingering, by switching to the B-flat horn, or by varying the position of the fingers of the right hand within the bell of the horn. The effective hand positions are open, half-stopped, three-quarters stopped, and fully stopped.

"For successful practicing on the horn, one should begin early with the lip slurs and also develop the use of the vowels in the throat ('ee', 'oo' as in 'Boo!', 'oh', and 'aw') and by taking the first steps on the long road to efficiency in the transpositions." Example 41 deals with the lip slur.

EXAMPLE 41. The lip slur

The notes given in the example appear in many variations, repetitions, and positions relative to each other. Soon, the upper F is added to the series, and the routines are repeated in an expanded form.

To bring transposition into the mainstream, similar lip exercises are played on each valve. Starting with the B-flat horn and adding valves, the exercise of Example 41 is lowered by half steps from the given F down to the C-sharp below. Then, changing to the F horn, the process is continued down from middle C to the lower F-sharp.

The student's ear is trained to become familiar with these changes in pitch right from the beginning. Much of the fear generated by the word transposition is eliminated.

Another recommendation for horn practice should be mentioned: *Learn to sing the exercises before playing them on the horn.* The only way to be utterly secure is to hear the desired pitch in the mind before calling it forth from the instrument. This facet of horn study is closely allied with practice on the strings. The latter have only the ear to depend upon for accuracy of intonation. Stout insists on his students being able to sing their exercises.

The proof of the methods of this duly famous teacher is the fact that he has so many former students scattered around the United States in the professional symphony orchestras. They shine in their familiarity with the transpositions and by their security in sight-reading as well as their sought-after tone quality.

Trumpet/cornet: The close relationship of one brass instrument to another is apparent. These two instruments are built in B-flat. There is a soprano cornet in E-flat that is often used in all-brass bands.

The trumpet in B-flat is used for band performance. (Band music is usually written in the flat keys.) The C trumpet is currently favored by professional players in major symphony orchestras.

Clifford Lillya, who served as solo cornet player in Bachman's "Million Dollar Band," stressed early emphasis on the lip slur (example taken from Lillya's *Method for Cornet and Trumpet.*)

EXAMPLE 42. Lip slur examples from *Method for Cornet and Trumpet* by Clifford Lillya, © 1937 M.M. Cole.

(A)   (B)

Commenting on item B in Example 42, Lillya said, "It is also good practice to hold the first valve down while adding the second valve, making it a reiteration study that is beneficial both for the ear and the fingers."

There are times in the studio when a teacher's use of a descriptive word gives the student the exact feeling for the technique itself. Speaking of the lip slur and using an arpeggio as the vehicle, Lillya says: "Cultivate a *slippery feeling* in the lip slurs."

EXAMPLE 43. Developing technique

He continues, "Start with an arpeggio on G; then go to an A-flat arpeggio. Play these with all seven fingering combinations."

Much of the artistry in trumpet/cornet performance relates to the use of the first and third slides, the "thumb slide" on the first valve, and the ring-finger slide on the third valve. No adjustments, while playing, are possible with the second valve.

"Whenever possible, adjust the intonation of the low C-sharp and D by extending the first- and third-valve slides."

To use the slides effectively, "Make the adjustment during a rest while taking a breath. A clumsy use of the slide, moving it simultaneously while activating the valve, might create a vacuum."

A common exercise for the wind instrumentalist is the "slur two, tongue two" with its reversal. When applied to a long etude that is entirely in eighths or sixteenths, many variations are possible.

EXAMPLE 44. Slur two, tongue two

Use A for several lines, then B for the next few lines, and so on with C and D. This will keep the mind functioning and fend off monotony.

Before leaving this section of the discussion, the tone quality of the trumpet, cornet, and the larger fluegelhorn should be mentioned. The trumpet is, above all else, brilliant—and the first choice for the symphony orchestra. The cornet is preferred for solo playing because of its more lyrical sound quality. The fluegelhorn has a darker sound. It is used in jazz music, but seldom chosen for use in the concert band.

Trombone: Here we have the utterly unique instrument—no fingering, no valves, just tubing that changes length to produce the pitches.

Glenn Smith of the heavenly tone speaks of legato tonguing: "The teachers of younger students are especially urged to emphasize this technique…as it can be accomplished at the beginning stages when slurring is first introduced. There are comparatively few 'natural' slurs on the trombone. A natural slur occurs when the slide and the pitches of the notes move in contrary motion.

EXAMPLE 45. The slide lengthens, but a higher note is sounded

Smith continues, "In playing a slurred passage, a soft stroke of the tongue is necessary to break the air column sufficiently to produce a smooth, clean separation of consecutive tones. After attacking the first tones of a slurred group in the usual manner, the following notes must be articulated by the repetition of either the syllable 'rah' or 'dah' as the flow of the breath is continued. The gentle stroke of the tongue is in the back of the teeth, touching the roof of the mouth. The 'rah' is more difficult to perfect but may prove more satisfactory in the end. The action of the tongue is much like that of a continuous rolling of the letter 'r,' refined to produce just one roll of the 'r.'"

The legato tongue action is to be practiced in slow, one-count intervals on sustained pitches in the middle register. Later it is applied to one-octave scales, using half-, quarter-, and eighth-note tempos. "Ten minutes of daily practice is recommended on this type of tonguing," Smith says.

The notes are spaced on the slide thus: between first and second positions, from 3.25 to 4.5 inches between sixth and seventh positions.

"Do not permit the habit of extending the fingers to touch the bell rim as a guide to third and fourth positions," Smith warns.

Regarding intonation, the reader may remember the discussion of the intonation problem in using the seventh partial.

Smith says, "The trombonist is the only brass instrumentalist who can utilize the seventh partial to any extent. The G4 (third line above the bass clef staff) and the neighboring F-sharp in this series are regularly played in the sharp second and the sharp third positions, respectively. F-natural is also used considerably by many trombonists as an alternate position in the raised fourth position. These notes are naturally extremely flat and, therefore, must be shortened more than is required to adjust the pitch in any other overtone series.

"Alternate positions help to facilitate the technique. D4 is probably (or should be) the most-used alternate position. The slide has to be lowered a little since this is the sixth partial, which has a tendency to be sharp. This same pitch (D4) is a little flat in the first position, and, therefore, some prefer to regularly use the fourth position for sustained tones.

"Efficient slide manipulation is the primary function of alternate positions. However, another purpose is also served—that of giving greater opportunities for natural slurs and lip slur combinations."

Euphonium: Fritz Kaenzig, principal tubist of Chicago's famous Grant Park Summer Concert Series, says, "The second-most popular solo instrument in the top professional bands at the turn of the century was the euphonium. When used in the symphony orchestra (as in some of Strauss's and Mahler's works) it is designated as the tenor tuba. The range is roughly that of the trombone, and it possesses a lovely tone plus a capacity for tremendous technique."

Tuba: That great big beautiful hunk of brass that supports the whole performance when permitted to participate, it adds its power and amplification to the string bass section in the symphony orchestra and "sets the rhythm" in the band.

There is nothing more dramatic than a descending scale in the tuba as it plumbs the depths—down, down, down to the center of the earth. It is a pity that too many times this fact is disregarded in the performance. But there is also a physical reason for it: *The lower the note, the greater the amount of air needed to produce the note.*

"The player's breath is not unlimited. There are times when his breath just gives out!—especially if he has to hold a low note for any long, loud duration," Kaenzig says.

He speaks of the tuba in these words: "One of the most surprising characteristics of the tuba is its ability to weave beautiful, resonant, lyrical melodies. To this end, most tuba teachers today require their students to play nineteenth-century *bel canto* vocalises daily, concentrating on beautiful tone, line, and phrasing. It is important for tubists to use breathing exercises as part of their customary daily practice. Likewise, they must stay in good physical shape to fully use their natural lung capacity.

"The distinguishing feature of tuba technique is the enormous amount of breath the player has to expend just to create the low-pitched lip buzz that causes the sound—a sound that is amplified by the almost sixteen-foot length of the tuba itself.

"In tone production, the idea is to get to the vowels as soon as possible. Consonants activate the tongue: thus, in starting the tone their role will be very short, so as to allow the vowel (and the freely flowing wind) to dominate. It takes a great impulse of wind to create immediate and specific low-frequency pitches. It is helpful to think a 'ho' following a brief but pure 't'-start to every tongued note."

"One must hear the desired tone quality and the exact pitch in advance of any efforts to produce sound on the tuba (for comparison, see French horn, pp. 97–99). Take in the fullest breath possible; then blow the wind necessary to realize that desired pitch and tone. Centering immediately on precise pitch is one of the great shortcomings on the tuba," Kaenzig says.

"The higher the pitch, the faster the air. The lower the pitch, the slower the air—but much more quantity will be needed.

"To activate these sounds, the player has to throw caution to the winds and use what breath he or she can muster just to get the tone started. While it takes courage and wind power, it also makes the breath conservation problem doubly difficult for the tubist."

Kaenzig is a well-known tuba soloist (although he himself says the tuba is not a solo instrument). He subscribes to what Louis Stout says about practicing the lower range: it is absolutely necessary.

Quoting Kaenzig one last time: "Practicing slowly, in order to actually hear and sound each individual note, is crucial to good technique. It is also important to separate the problem spots or 'cells' from the rest of the material and to practice those cells slowly, accurately, and repetitively. Using alternate rhythms with the same pitches as those in the problem spots is a great practice tool."

Chapter Thirteen

The Strings: Violin, Viola, Cello, String Bass

The quickest way to produce a sound from a string under tension is to pluck it—to pull it aside and release it. The technical term is *pizzicato*.

The *pizzicato*: There is an interesting (but unhappy) phenomenon taking place today in performances by the symphony orchestras, be they professional or amateur. As audiences, we are not hearing the *pizzicato* notes clearly, although we can *see* them being performed. *Pizzicato* passages are being treated too casually.

The *pizzicato* is notated for one of several reasons: first, for its own intrinsic value; second, to highlight one or more special notes being played by another instrument where a written accent would be too obvious; and third, to serve as an exclamation point, either *pianissimo* as in the *Der Freischütz* Overture by Carl Maria von Weber or for *fortissimo* as on a particular note in the opera *La bohème* by Giacomo Puccini, where it can never be played loudly enough to please the conductor.

The *pizzicato* technique: Here is where the harp reigns supreme. Almost the first thing a harp student learns at the very first lesson is this: Hook the thumb over a string and then pull (pluck) another string with the first, second, or third finger. The placement of the thumb is to furnish a point of resistance for the other fingers to pull against. If the thumb itself has to pluck, then the third finger sets itself to form the point of resistance on a lower-pitched string. The harp technique concerns itself with the thumb and three fingers on each hand.

In former days, a similar thing went on in the violin lesson. For *pizzicatos*, the thumb was allowed to release its grip on the bow and the frog of the bow settled into the fist of the player. The thumb then set itself along the side of the fingerboard to furnish a point of resistance for the plucking fingers. The plucking is cleaner when it has to overcome resistance.

Today we see many passages of *pizzicato* being played with the bow hand still in playing position. The first finger sticks out into the air and pulls on the string upwards. The result is a faked *pizzicato* sound that is more visual than audible.

The next bit on *pizzicato* has to do with the left hand. Finger pressure should not relax the instant the plucking finger finishes its plucking stroke. A plucked note will retain its resonance longer if the left-hand finger maintains its contact with the string touching the fingerboard.

Finally, I will mention the twisting of the string (slightly) as it is plucked. This is best described as a technique of flattening the plucking finger and starting the stroke by laying the finger flat on the string (about at the finger's first joint) and pulling it across the string as if bowing the string. This twists the string slightly. It is a recommended technique that works beautifully on the longer strings of the viola when richness of sound is desired.

It is possible that as everything sped up during the end of the twentieth century, the players just saved time by not bothering to use the original *pizzicato* technique. But it still produces the best result.

The fingering system: To finger any of the stringed instruments, fingers are placed consecutively to shorten the string and raise its pitch. On violin and viola, consecutive fingers produce scale sequences. On cello, the second and third fingers produce half steps. The string bass uses only first, second, and fourth fingers. The third finger is omitted in the lower positions because of the size of the instrument. Fingers one and two are a half step, and fingers two and four form a second half step; thus, one to four is one whole tone.

Pitches: The double bass sounds an octave lower than the cello when reading the same notation. The cello is considered to be the real bass of the orchestra. The viola is tuned an octave above the cello. (See p. 111 for the viola clef.)

The seven positions: This refers to the position of the left hand as it climbs up (violin/viola) or moves down (cello/bass) the neck of the instrument going *toward* the bridge.

Placing the first finger on any one of the strings and moving the finger ahead on the string (or the hand on the neck of the instrument) for seven steps produces a complete scale on that string. Use your ear to tune the seven notes. This locates the seven positions. In each of these seven positions, the violinist and the violist can play a two-octave-plus-one-note scale by crossing from one string to the next in the process. (It amounts, finger-wise, to the wind player's knowledge of transposition into other keys, but it is much easier and more facile on the strings.) Each finger on the violin and viola can play its pitch plus the sharp and the flat of that pitch in every position.

The cello also uses the seven positions but cannot form a complete scale because of the half-step relationship of the second and third fingers.

The double bass uses the half steps as intermediaries between the whole tones in numbering the positions: half position, first position, one and one-half, two, etc., as the scale progresses. Numbered from the A string, the numberings are the same on all four instruments: notes are all naturals, and there are no accidentals when numbering the positions.

Tone color and dynamics: To change the color and the dynamics, pay attention to the bow's speed of stroke, its pressure on the string, and its distance from the bridge—a three-way control. Closer to the bridge, heavy pressure and slower speed produce *fortes*. Closer to the fingerboard, lighter pressure and faster speed produce soft dynamics. Color is correspondingly affected.

Harmonics: The technical name for an overtone, as played on the strings, is a *harmonic*. The stringed instruments can bring into audible range the overtones that form the tonal color. Tonal color is comprised of the number of overtones present and their relative strengths. Harmonics are designated as either "natural" or "artificial."

The natural overtone is produced thus: While bowing the string, touch it *lightly* with a finger at one-half of its length from open string to bridge. The open string is the "fundamental." The note produced at the halfway point is the octave of the fundamental just as it is in the overtone series.

Touch the string at one-third its length from either end of the string, and the next overtone sounds the fifth above. Then, at one-quarter of its length, the double octave is heard. One-fifth of the string is sometimes used, but this is rather dangerous on the smaller instruments.

Cello and bass use these "natural harmonics" very freely at the bridge-end of the fingerboard with the thumb and the first three fingers.

The artificial harmonics: Any note on the violin, viola, or cello can be turned into a harmonic. To do this, the first finger (or thumb on cello) presses the string down firmly onto the fingerboard. Then the fourth finger (third usually on cello) touches the *same string* lightly at one-quarter of the remaining distance to the bridge. The note held down by the first finger (or thumb) will be heard as a harmonic two octaves above the note.

To bow the harmonics, stay away from the fingerboard and play nearer the bridge with "sufficient pressure to make a good tone on an *open* string." (The quote is from Ivan Galamian.) The bow at that place on the string moves more slowly and heavily.

Yes, the string technique is almost infinite—and yet simple enough that three-year-olds learn to play their little solos very nicely. All it takes to arrive eventually is years of love for the instrument, a personal desire to succeed, and (you guessed it!) practice, practice, practice. Without the strings there would be no symphony orchestra—no Fifth and all the rest of that magnificent repertoire. What a loss to the world! Then, too, we must remember that "it takes two." Without the artistry of the great wind soloists, their fascinating colors could not emerge to our delight during the symphony performances.

Everything finally comes together in the symphonic repertoire. Long may it live!

DIAGRAM 2. The basic principle of all bowing is this: The bow moves "straight" across the string, forming a right angle with the string. It seems simple enough—except that it does not quite work out that way.

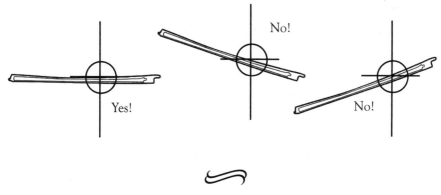

Violin/viola: Notice that when the arm is bent at the elbow, the lower arm can move easily to the left and to the right and can bend upward or return downward. But in so doing the motion is circular in character. In any motion of the arm itself, be it from elbow or from the shoulder, the extremity (the hand) is describing part of a circle. It is not moving in a straight line.

With the instrument in playing position and the bow resting on the string at the frog, the bow moves easily to its midpoint. It is easy to keep the straight line functioning. When the bow is on the string at its midpoint, the normal arm is bent to form a right angle at the elbow (see Diagram 3, point C).

DIAGRAM 3. D shows forward motion of the upper arm to produce A

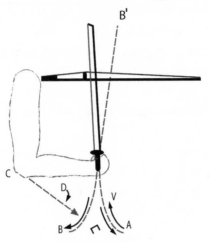

As the bow moves from its midpoint to its tip, the arm opens up and begins its circular motion. This starts to upset the straight line for the bow (line B–B' in the diagram). Therefore, the backward swinging circular motion (C) must be negated by a similar forward motion in the arm (line A in the diagram). This is the correct motion to produce the straight line in the bow stroke. The up-bow, starting at the point, *retraces line A exactly* as it returns to its midpoint. That little forward swing as the downstroke progresses was the secret, if there was any, to Galamian's ability to improve the player's sound within the first two weeks of study in his studio. It gives the bow a "straight" attack at the point instead of a slanting attack. (Note: There are a few people with long arms who need very little of the forward push on the down-bow.)

The preceding skill requires on viola longer stretch of the arm at the point of the bow than it does on the violin. It is not unusual to hear violists mention a "tired arm" after a long, intense rehearsal.

Violas come in 14-, 15-, 16-, and 17-inch sizes together with the half-inch additions. Violinists often make the mistake of buying the 14-inch instrument "so as not to upset their violin intonation."

Actually, this is the wrong approach for two reasons. First, the difference in finger placement is too small to be easily conquered, and the intonation suffers on *both* instruments. Second, one will never experience the true viola sound on the small instrument. There is a definite mathematical relationship for resonance that has to do with the relative lengths of the instrument and the lowest sound wave (pitch) it must produce. This relationship is *approximated* in 16- and 17-inch violas, but if the relationship were perfect, the viola would be too long to be playable. (Note: A professor at Northwestern University had such an instrument built as an experiment. No one could get the fingers onto the strings except by setting the instrument on his or her knees and playing it like a cello.) It is suggested by fine viola players to use the bow just a bit closer to the bridge than is customary on the violin.

Becoming familiar with the viola clef—the "alto" clef—is not as difficult as it seems. Several tricks can help. The middle line of the clef is middle C. Everything above that line comes from the treble clef; everything below the C line is bass clef. The two lines above middle C are the two bottom lines of the treble clef. The two lines below C are the two top lines of the bass clef. To read the alto clef as if it had a treble clef signature, add the next higher letter name to the name of the printed note. Then drop it an octave to get the exact pitch that is being sounded. Middle-line printed treble-clef B is C an octave lower.

For instant reading coming from violin to viola, place the hand in first position on the viola, but finger each line and each space as if you were reading third position, treble clef, on the violin. Third line on the staff (in third position) is the third finger on the third string of the instrument. Just read automatically, and let your ear establish the key. *But do not stop here.* Making use of the shortcut, momentarily, does not excuse you from learning the clef properly.

Return to being a real musician by playing the clef on the piano until you are clear as to what pitches you are reading (Note: This method is absolute horror to certain fine musicians—bless them!—but it accomplishes in twenty minutes what otherwise takes a couple of weeks. It turns a good violinist into a string quartet violist as soon as he or she catches on to the trick. A new quartet materializes without waiting to find a viola player. The new violist improves rapidly. Fact: It took Joseph Gingold just ten minutes to teach Pinchas Zukerman to read the viola clef when Pinchas was about fourteen. It is very easy to fall in love with the viola.)

Cello: There is a serious fault that one sees occurring throughout the United States among the very young players of the cello (and the bass). It is probably due to the fact that real cellists are not as numerous as violinists who teach cello.

When the bow is on the string in playing position, the students tend to hold it so that the bow stick is directly opposite the hair *horizontally*. This negates any possibility of drawing a good, rich cello tone. Any pressure the student applies to the bow simply drops off into the air below the horizontal stick. It never gets to the string.

The proper position for the bow is to have the stick perpendicular to and above the hair. In other words, the inner edge of the bow hair is what should contact the string. Pressure then broadens the hair contact and produces good tonal results.

It takes only a few moments to correct this fault. The student quickly finds that he or she can produce a really satisfactory tone.

String bass: The above paragraphs concerning the cello bow are equally applicable to the bass. Bassists taught by non-bassists have an identical problem. The simple remedy of using the inner edge of the hair as the contact point forces the stick to right itself.

There are several other points to make for the bassist. If he or she is using the "French" bow, then cello technique is applicable. The two bows are held in much the same manner. But if the "German" bow is used, then things are totally different.

Which bow is better? Experts disagree, but there are more French bows in use in the symphonies than German. The French bow makes the *spiccato* easier to execute, and the players appear to be more relaxed with it. But there is also justification for using the German bow.

The French bow has one point of leverage; it exists between the thumb beneath the frog and the first and third fingers on the far side of the frog.

The German bow has two points of leverage: the thumb on top of the stick, with the extended frog between it and the first finger, forms one lever—a powerful one. The thumb pressure feeds directly into the string. A second lever exists between the thumb and the two fingers opposite that rest on the stick. As the fingers push inward, the thumb again pushes downward, producing the second type of leverage. In this latter case, the fingers-and-bow response is similar to that of the French bow.

The German bow has the "added mileage" of the downward pressure in the thumb. This is not true of the French bow. It appears to be a fact that much of the richness of that low bass line, doubling the cellos in the lower octave, is missing today in the professional orchestral sound. Perhaps this massive old bass needs the massive old grip on the bow to be efficient. Who knows? At the end of the nineteenth century, there was a very famous Hungarian bass soloist who had a way of presenting the German bow technique that has been handed down for a couple of generations. It was as follows:

Place bow on string. Then, four steps: 1. STOP! 2. Wrist 3. Press bow into string (leverage). 4. Release, pressure, and play. Same thing at the point of the bow: stop/wrist/press/release and play.

This accomplishes two things: A fine contact of the bow with the strings and a very flexible wrist that is of immense comfort to the player in tremolo passages. The wrist action takes place at every change of direction in the bow stroke.

The wrist action spoken of above is this: For the down-bow, the hand bends exaggeratedly toward the right so that the wrist precedes the hand all the way. In making this change of position, the fingers temporarily lose contact with their correct playing position. (They resume correct position as the technique becomes easy.)

For the up-bow from the point, the hand completely reverses its position. It now makes a right angle with the arm, fingers pointing to the left; and the square wrist pulls or leads the hand back to the frog. The fingers are parallel with the bow's length.

The "STOP!" gives the player time to adjust the hand-wrist combination each time before playing.

The "press" makes the necessary solid contact of bow with thick, heavy bass string. *It affects the entire length of the string.* When the bow finally moves, it takes the whole string with it. When the initial bow pressure is too weak, the string sometimes forms the octave harmonic, vibrating in two halves and delivering the insipid tone too often heard. The "release" lets the bow move without producing a miserable scratchy sound. When the pressure lets up, the string "bounces" back, its entire length under control of the bow.

The motion of the bass bow starts from the shoulder. The elbow bend is missing; the full arm moves the bow. The flexible wrist is the "trick" for the German bow.

There is one other hint for the bass player. This one comes from Anton Torello Sr., principal bassist for the Philadelphia Orchestra for a great many years. He also taught at the Curtis Institute. In due time, both of his sons became members of the Philadelphia bass section. The information that follows is unique, based as it is on the Torello expertise, and deals with the dynamics of the bass *pizzicato*: "The softest place to pluck the bass string is at its midpoint between finger and bridge. The string is most flexible there, and the vibration will continue the longest.

"The next loudest place to pluck is at the bridge-end of the fingerboard. The string is stiffer here, and the energy is directed toward the bridge. The vibration does not last as long.

"For the loudest possible *pizzicato*, pluck right next to the finger that is holding down the note."

This information is helpful also to the band conductor when he wants to hear that little four-note descending scale, written so often midway in the trio of a march. This is the one place where the string bass can actually be heard.

PART THREE:
SCIENCE AND TEACHING

Chapter Fourteen

The Brain and the Learning Process

It is imperative today that practicing musicians—students, teachers, professional performers—have some understanding of the remarkable discoveries concerning the brain and its learning processes that were made during the second half of the tremendous twentieth century. Since 1950, brain research has exploded.

The human brain is comprised of two mirrored halves—the left brain and the right brain—which are similar in structure but differ in certain functions.

Many years ago it became apparent that an injury in one half of the brain resulted in paralysis in the *opposite* side of the body. This brought with it the realization that the right brain controls the left hand and the left brain manages the right hand.

The two halves of the brain are connected by a mass of fibers called the *corpus callosum*. Its purpose is to correlate the two halves.

The brain also contains some 30–40 billion cells. These cells are connected and interconnected. When we learn something new, the cells that are designated as neurons begin to show activity. They start to reach toward other cells in order to establish a new pathway in the brain.

As we practice, we strengthen the new pathway we have established. When we have made it strong enough, we find that it has become a habit and will work automatically.

This is the basic reason for *not* making mistakes when we practice. We simply confuse the neurons. How does all of this affect our manual technique in learning to play an instrument?

The thought, or command initiated in the brain, travels through the "neural pathway" to our hands (or whatever we wish to use). The neural pathway is described as similar to a series of hyphens (- - - - - -). The electrical charge initiated by the brain starts down the neural pathway. When it comes to one of the spaces, two (or more) chemicals form automatically to carry the impulse across the gap. This trip from brain to hands works instantaneously. The thought precedes the response, but the response becomes instantaneous.

All of this brings us to the basic philosophy on which this book is founded: *think first—before you play it wrong.*

Two things have emerged: First, *slow practice is imperative.* (This is endorsed by every good teacher. It is not news to any of you who are reading this book.)

"Take time to think" is basic. We must not force the student to "think fast"—and play it wrong. We must, instead, *plan for the child to have time to think.* This explains the fermata-rest.

The second thing that emerged was the careful outlining certain of the celebrated authorities presented in their interviews. Oboe and bassoon teachers, particularly, set up the thinking process for the beginner at the very first lesson.

Once the habit of thinking first is established, it will gradually speed up. When it does, we can then worry about "getting there on the next beat"—but still with accuracy.

For suggestions on ways to accomplish these first steps, see the next chapter. Its description of the introduction to etude practice may be helpful. To "play each note four times" in the early lessons crops up again on p. 124; this slows down the reading process and gives the mind time to think.

A final word on the brain: it is far more flexible than researchers first realized.

The most amazing thing is that when an activity has been continued for years, its path is so firmly established that its skills can once again be enlivened, even after years of neglect, if the effort is accompanied by infinite patience.

Here is the most astonishing statement of all: The number of possible connections in the brain is greater than the number of atoms in the universe. In other words, we have infinite power at our disposal. All we have to do is to learn to use it. The following quotation comes from Ivan Galamian's *Principles of Violin Playing and Teaching*. (To make it applicable to any musical instrumental, simply omit the word violin as you read it.)

> The key to facility and accuracy, and ultimately to complete mastery of the violin technique is to be found in the relationship of mind to muscles, that is, in the ability to make the sequence of mental command and physical response as quick and precise as possible. Therein resides the fundamental principle of violin technique that is being overlooked by far too many players and teachers.

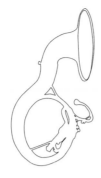

Chapter Fifteen

Introducing the Child to Serious Practice

During the 1970s, Dr. Mihaly Csikszentmihalyi, professor of psychology at the University of Chicago, became intrigued by the fact that there are among us certain individuals who can sustain their concentration on a task during extraordinarily long periods of time. Doctors engaged in brain surgery (seven or more hours); athletes running in marathon races; and artists and musicians involved in their creative activities are all examples. The passing of time ceases to exist in their consciousness. Csikszentmihalyi called this state "the Flow." His conclusions, in brief, are these:

- When the challenge and variety inherent in the task are matched by the ability of the performer, then the phenomenon of the Flow can occur.
- When the task is too difficult for the ability of the participant, frustration occurs.
- When the ability of the participant is greater than the demands of the task, boredom sets in.

Fine dividends will accrue if we keep in mind the three conclusions stated by Dr. Csikszentmihalyi and apply them in our practicing and teaching.

In today's society, the child's first instrumental music lessons are likely to come from the classes provided by many of the public schools as part of their elective curriculum. Classes taught by music specialists usually produce fine results. But some classes are taught by non-specialists, and their students may acquire (unintentionally) certain firmly established bad habits that must be corrected.

By the end of the first year, the aspiring young musicians have learned to produce tone on their chosen instruments, to finger certain notes, perhaps to read music, and certainly to play a few favorite tunes. (If piano is the chosen instrument, each hand has been trained individually and, thereafter, to work together.)

Whatever the situation may be, the youngsters should be introduced to "serious" practice, be it corrective or otherwise, during their second year of study.

This second year, either in classes or in private lessons, is then devoted to refining the accomplishments of the introductory year, building on the enthusiasm engendered in the classes.

Learning to practice: Let us now identify with Bobby, who has chosen to play clarinet, and Jimmy, whose love is the violin.

As a player of a wind instrument, Bobby will be dealing with enhancing his breath control, the mechanism that produces his sound. He will be using simple notes and short slurs. He will not be repetitiously tonguing the same note. Sustaining the sound is more important.

Jimmy, playing a stringed instrument (violin, viola, cello, or string bass), will spend his time improving his skill with the bow stroke. He *will* be repeating single notes in succession, giving him time to concentrate on the stroke itself.

The short etudes will progress by easy steps. Bobby will come across some repetitive finger patterns, and Johnny will encounter some basic bowing patterns. Both boys will gradually become interested in practicing if variety is included in the assignment. To do something simple in several ways provides a challenge. As each small "problem" is undertaken and successfully conquered, the child realizes that he himself has made progress, which is a great feeling at the end of a practice session.

As teachers, we must study to *create* the small problems that will challenge the student and be indicative of progress. And these problems must be presented on the child's level. The problems must accompany the assignment when we make it.

Jimmy will have a longer road to travel because each hand is engaged in a different type of activity. The left hand sets the notes to be sounded; and the right hand sounds them with the long, unwieldy bow. Jimmy will have to think while he practices, and he will have to notice, consciously, what his bow stroke is doing.

Both will be using their ears to recognize the correct pitch when it happens. Bobby gets some help from the fingering—cover the right holes, and a certain note will sound. Jimmy has no such luck. Only his ear can tell him if he has played the correct pitch. Bobby listens for tone. Jimmy listens for pitch. Good practice habits depend upon what the student actually hears.

When Jimmy starts his second year of string playing, he takes his first private lesson. Suddenly, Jimmy is confronted by a whole page of black notes, eight to the bar. ("Gee!")

EXAMPLE 46. Eighth note passage

They look ominous, and there are too many of them. He knows immediately that his powers are not yet developed enough to deal with what appears to be a formidable (and perhaps boring) task. Jimmy looks frightened.

But Jimmy's teacher will take care of the problems. She knows that reiteration is imperative—"thirty minutes to an hour each day." However, assigning that amount of practice time is of meager value.

Psychologically, it focuses the child's attention on the clock instead of on the goal to be achieved.

So the teacher smooths Jimmy's path by *adjusting the assignment to fit the student's ability.*

"Jimmy, you are going to spend several lessons on this page. You will not have to play it all in one week. This is how it works.

"You will practice just *one* line each day. Start with the first line and play each note four times: down, up, down, up using only half of the bow from the frog to the middle and up-bowing to the frog again."

(This immediately slows down the reading process as well as the practice tempo and gives Jimmy a chance to dwell on each pitch long enough to *hear* it.) The first important step in serious practice is to give the ear an opportunity to hear exactly how the sequence of notes should sound.

The teacher continues: "I'll put a white chalk dot on the stick of the bow at the middle. Start at the frog and tip the bow onto the *outer* edge of the hair. By the time you get to the white dot, the full hair surface may be on the string. This is good." (Note: It is the same for the viola, but the cello and the double bass use the bow on the inner edge of the hair. The stick of the bow is perpendicularly *above* the hair, *not horizontally opposite it*—as is too often seen among young cellists and bassists.)

To continue: "When you can do this well, then start at the middle of the bow, and go to the point, four times on each note, still on the first line of music. Remember to reach forward as you approach the point on the down-bow, and retract the reach as the up-bow gets underway. Use just that half of the bow."

So what of Bobby during this time? Bobby has been mixing short slurs with longer sustained notes, playing each two-measure phrase twice. On an exercise similar to Jimmy's repetitions, Bobby has been adding short slurs interspersed with longer half notes.

In any case, the goal has been to concentrate on the uninterrupted, continuous sound while notes change. The students are not allowed to leave the studio until each has demonstrated that he understands how to practice the lesson.

Each child has been given more than one way to practice his lesson and each understands the specific goal for the week.

By suggesting several ways to practice, reiteration is built into the assignment. When Jimmy plays each note four times, the problem is made easy. By making it easy, the teacher inveigles Jimmy to draw his good bow stroke 160 times on each line of music. (Eight notes to the bar, five measures to the line: forty notes. Play each note four times and one hundred and sixty bows have been drawn. You'd never get this many bowings by assigning a half hour of practice for each day.)

And our Jimmy comes bouncing in at the next lesson: "Gee! It's fun to practice that way!"

In actuality, Jimmy has embarked on a month's study of the eight fundamental bowings. In the second week, the problem is to connect those two well-rehearsed bow halves into one long, smooth bow stroke. The assigned exercise is Example 47.

EXAMPLE 47. The long, smooth bow stroke

Jimmy links these halves together: a) frog to middle *think* "stop at the middle," b) middle to point *think* "forward to the point," c) point to middle *think* "retract the forward reach"; and d) middle to frog *think* "on the edge of the hair to the frog."

To eliminate the stop as the bow moves smoothly from frog to point, see that it follows its practiced path. *Each written note is now played only one time using a whole bow.*

About this time, the practicing for winds and strings begins to correlate—slurs interspersed with unslurred notes. Probably the most often encountered form is that given in the next example.

EXAMPLE 48. With bowings

Each note is played one at a time. Use whole bow on the slurs and half-bows for the unslurred notes. This again combines the material from the previous lesson. The logical sequence is not upset. The fingers play the next written note every time the bow changes its direction.

The next pattern is applicable to winds and strings. It emphasizes rhythmic evenness in finger placement and embodies two important principles for the strings.

EXAMPLE 49. Exercise for rhythmic evenness

Strings, problem one: On a fast whole-bow, down-bow before a slur, and *exaggerate the forward reach.*

Problem two: On the fast up-bow, lift the bow OFF the strings as the frog is approached, and reset it at the frog for the next down-bow. This trains lightness into the fast up-stroke so that there is no dynamic change to the unwanted *forte* that so often is heard in school orchestras when this bowing problem is encountered. Later on, in fast playing, the lift will disappear, but the *forte* will not occur. Use the lift whenever necessary in performance.

With the conquering of these basic problems, a good foundation is laid for more advanced study. Perhaps it should be added that for the strings it has proved effective to assign one month of slow, careful, precise practice at the beginning of the second year of study. Typically, students progress faster during the months that follow.

Chapter Sixteen

Summary on Teaching

There are definite trends in teaching philosophy and in practice methods. The brain research mentioned in Chapter Fourteen has had an enormous impact in making us understand the unlimited power of that fabulous organ. To plug into that power is up to us. What we must have is a desire to know and the personal drive to satisfy that desire. We must be willing to strive for what we get in this world.

A gentleman named A. R. Cassavant said in 1960, "The possession of knowledge will raise a man to mediocrity but not to distinction," and, "The knowledge itself is less important than the inspiration it took to get it." Whether one accepts these opinions or not, at least they challenge one to pause a moment and think.

It is what we do with the knowledge after we get it that affects our world and our relationship to it. The open mind, the inquiring mind, is humankind's greatest wealth.

The educational trends that have emerged in the interviews with our music experts stress, more and more, that we must be sure as teachers that our students really understand what we are teaching. The knowledge of *how* to do it—*how* to begin to learn to play an instrument, *how* to start out, *how* to practice.

Some of the greatest teachers are setting their methods into logical teaching order—even the simple tasks of the very first lesson. And they are emphasizing that *once is not enough.* Complete each item four times. Set the embouchure four times. Here is a sample of such a stepwise approach: L. Hugh Cooper's outline. *Repeat each initiation four times before going on to the next note.*

Correct order of initiation:
1. Take a deep breath, using the abdominal muscles.
2. Place the tip of the reed on the tip of the tongue, thus closing the reed aperture and establishing the reed's correct depth in the mouth.
3. Shape the lips around the reed to form an embouchure and to establish a hermetic seal.
4. Build playing pressure in the oral cavity by using abdominal support. *Do not produce a sound or allow breath to pass through the reed or leak around it.*
5. Quickly withdraw the tongue from the reed, and a sound will begin.

"Try it!" This controlled approach will work on any reed instrument every time. (Notice the word "attack" does not appear anywhere in this discussion, hopefully establishing a trend.)

Paul Kantor (violinist), a member of the artist faculty at the Aspen (Colorado) Music Festival and School, spoke of his philosophy of teaching: "The slow practice is absolutely necessary, but—caution—it can also become a trap. It is necessary to play through up to tempo periodically in order to prevent the slow tempo from slowing down our overall thinking-doing process. Every once in a while, try it over tempo."

Kantor also expressed his conviction that "memorizing involves several different types of memory. It is not just one thing. There is an *intellectual memory*—as for the harmonic analysis—and a *tactile memory* that the hands, muscles, and body absorb as the repetitions grow. Memory is affected by familiar associations. The latter could be tested by taking a lovely melodic passage made up of notes of varying length and playing it through with every note the same length."

More than one of our experts spoke of "avoiding routines." Change from day to day the order of the repertoire, the particular scale to be practiced that day, the motifs to be used for the practice. Keep the mind alive and working.

Lawrence Hurst, professor of music (string bass) and chairman of the string department at Indiana University (Bloomington) is one of the great string bass teachers of the century. His career began as principal bassist of the Dallas Symphony with Georg Solti as the conductor. Hurst's thorough knowledge of the professional aspect of a musical career moved him to *prepare* his students for success in that field.

In order to get a degree in string bass, the applicant must play a graduation recital and also successfully pass a "thirty-minute examination in symphonic repertoire, performing *from memory*." (No wonder they get the jobs in every orchestra of repute, both in the United States and in Europe!)

As part of the training for the career, Hurst has them concentrate their practice on intervals. "Due to the character of the non-melodic parts, the intervallic practice is important. Scales in fifths and thirds form some of this practice." It also gives security in changing positions freely.

"Stay with one scale for a week, then choose another scale for the next week."

The trend is apparent in the graduate programs of the universities: giving the students personal contact with the finest of the professional players so that they are fully prepared for any auditions they may have to make. The authorities are those who have *lived the life*.

THE EXPERTS

Buyse, Leone: *Flute.* Leone Buyse is on the faculty of Rice University's Shepherd School of Music as professor of flute and chamber music. Previously professor of flute at the University of Michigan, she relinquished her position with the Boston Symphony Orchestra in 1993 to pursue a more active teaching and solo career after twenty-two years as an orchestral musician.

Acting principal flutist of the BSO since September 1990, she was invited by Seiji Ozawa to join the orchestra in 1983 as assistant principal flutist and principal flutist of the Boston Pops. Before moving to Boston, she served as assistant principal flutist of the San Francisco Symphony and played piccolo and flute with the Rochester Philharmonic Orchestra. The only American finalist in the 1969 Geneva International Flute Competition, Buyse has appeared as a soloist with numerous orchestras, including l'Orchestre de la Suisse Romande, the Boston Pops, the San Francisco Symphony, the Utah Symphony, the Rochester Philharmonic, and the New Hampshire Music Festival, of which she was principal flutist for ten years. She made her debut as soloist with the Boston Symphony at Tanglewood in August 1993, performing Leonard Bernstein's *Halil* under John Williams. As a member of the Webster Trio and the Buyse-Webster Duo she performs frequently with her husband, clarinetist Michael Webster.

Widely recognized as one of America's foremost flute pedagogues, Buyse has taught at the New England Conservatory, Boston University, Tanglewood Music Center, the Boston University Tanglewood Institute, and as a visiting associate professor at the Eastman School of Music. A native of Ithaca, New York, Buyse graduated with distinction from the Eastman School of Music, where she was a student of Joseph Mariano. Awarded a Fulbright grant, she subsequently studied in France with Michel Debost, Jean-Pierre Rampal, and Marcel Moyse. An active member of the National Flute Association, she has served on the Board of Directors, as coordinator of the Orchestral Audition and Master Class Competition, and as program chair for the 1987 convention in St. Louis.

Cooper, Lewis Hugh. *Bassoon.* Cooper was a member of the Detroit Symphony Orchestra from 1946–1964, performing in approximately 2,500 concerts and serving as bassoonist on more than 30 distinguished recordings made by the orchestra under the direction of Paul Paray (Mercury label).

Cooper has been a design consultant in the manufacture of bassoons to the firms of Josef Püchner-Holtblasinstrumentum, Germany and Oscar Adler-Blechblas Instrumentum, Germany. One of his major contributions to the bassoon world has been as an acoustician. Cooper Model bassoons are being successfully produced by both of the above makers and have established an international reputation for their musical excellence. During his more than fifty years of association as faculty at the University of Michigan, Cooper has given more than one hundred extracurricular concerts plus nearly two hundred lectures, clinics, and demonstrations, including international appearances in England, Scotland, Norway, Denmark, Germany, Austria, and Canada.

Hurst, Lawrence: *String bass.* Hurst is professor of music (double bass) and chairman of the String Department at Indiana University. He earned his bachelor's and master's degrees in music at the University of Michigan.

Hurst is the former principal double bassist of the Dallas Symphony. He was previously a faculty member of Southern Methodist and Eastern

Michigan Universities and former faculty member, associate dean, and chairman of the string department at University of Michigan School of Music. He was honored with the Alumni Award from the University of Michigan School of Music in 1998 and in 2005 received the Artist/Teacher of the Year Award from the American String Teachers Association.

Professor Hurst is former director of the University Division of the National Music Camp and is a summer faculty member of the Interlochen Arts Camp. He is past chairman of the American String Teachers Association National Solo Competition and past president of the International Society of Bassists. His former students can be found in many prestigious orchestras, including Chicago, Philadelphia, San Francisco, St. Louis, Indianapolis, the Met Opera Orchestra, and Atlanta.

Kaenzig, Fritz: *Tuba.* Kaenzig is professor of tuba and euphonium and chairman of the Wind and Percussion Department at the University of Michigan. He has served as principal tubist of the Florida Symphony Orchestra and as additional or substitute tubist with Amsterdam's Concertgebouw and the symphony orchestras of Detroit, San Francisco, Houston, Chicago, Los Angeles, and St. Louis, under such conductors as Bernstein, Haitink, Leinsdorf, Ozawa, Salonen, and Slatkin. He has also recorded and performed as a soloist with many of these and several others.

Since 1984, he has been principal tubist in the Grant Park (Chicago) Symphony Orchestra during summers. As guest instructor, recitalist, soloist with ensembles, and adjudicator, Kaenzig has made appearances at many high schools, colleges, universities, conferences, and music camps throughout the United States, Korea, and Japan. Prior to joining the faculty in 1989, he taught at the University of Illinois and the University of Northern Iowa in Cedar Falls. Kaenzig graduated from Ohio State University and the University of Wisconsin at Madison and was a member of the Tanglewood Music Center Orchestra. He is past president of the Tubists Universal Brotherhood Association, now known as the International Tuba and Euphonium Association, which he currently serves as a member of the Board of Directors and as a frequently featured soloist at its international conferences.

Kantor, Paul: *Violin*. Kantor is the Eleanor H. Biggs Memorial Distinguished Professor of Violin at the Cleveland Institute of Music. He earned bachelor's and master's degrees from the Juilliard School. His principal teachers include Margaret Graves, Dorothy DeLay, and Robert Mann. Kantor served as chairman of the string department at the University of Michigan for thirteen years.

As a chamber musician, he has performed with the New York String Quartet, Berkshire Chamber Players, Lenox Quartet, and the National Musical Arts Chamber Ensemble. Kantor served as concertmaster of the New Haven Symphony, Aspen Chamber Symphony and Festival Orchestra, Lausanne Chamber Orchestra, and Great Lakes Festival Orchestra and as guest concertmaster of the New Japan Philharmonic and the Toledo Symphony Orchestra. His former teaching positions include those at Yale University (1981–88), the New England Conservatory (1984–88), and the Juilliard School (1985–88). Kantor has been a member of the artist-faculty at Aspen since 1980. His world premiere performances include Dan Welcher's Violin Concerto and John Corigliano's *Red Violin Caprices*. Kantor has recorded for Equilibrium, CRI, Delos, and Mark Records.

Lillya, Clifford: *Trumpet, cornet*. Lillya was solo cornet player for the Bachman Million Dollar Band. He had years of influence on the teaching of trumpet and cornet in the United States. His publications have been used in the beginning classes in many regions of the country (*Method for Cornet and Trumpet*). His *Trumpet (Cornet) Technic*, originally copyrighted in 1952 by Carl Fischer, gives a summary of basic skills, applied music theory, orchestra and band routines, and recital and chamber music literature.

Lillya's former students hold positions in the Philadelphia Orchestra (associate principal trumpet), the Chicago Symphony, the Los Angeles Symphony, and the Baltimore Symphony. Lillya was professor emeritus of the University of Michigan School of Music. He was on the faculty for thirty-two years.

Sargous, Harry: *Oboe.* Sargous has been a guest artist with many orchestras in the United States and Canada, a guest soloist on CBC Radio and Television, BBC London, WDR Koln, Swedish Rijksradio, and a recitalist in North America, Europe, and Japan. He has shared the stage as a soloist with many prominent artists, including the late David Oistrakh. He made his Carnegie Hall debut to critical acclaim.

For several summers, Sargous performed at the renowned Marlboro Festival as principal oboist in the orchestra conducted by Pablo Casals. Former faculty positions include professor of music at the University of Michigan; the Royal Conservatory of Music, Toronto; The University of Western Ontario; and the University of Toronto.

Sinta, Donald: *Saxophone.* Sinta is chairman of the Winds Department at the University of Michigan, where he joined the faculty in 1974. Formerly on the faculties of the Hartt School of Music and Ithaca College, he is active as a soloist and clinician throughout the United States and Canada. His recording *American Music for the Saxophone* is known throughout the world.

Sinta has premiered more than forty works by American composers, and in 1969 he was the first elected chair of the World Saxophone Congress. He is director of the All-State Program at Interlochen and the Michigan Youth Ensembles Program. Sinta held an Arthur Thurnau Professorship, an award for outstanding instruction at the undergraduate level, and is the Earl V. Moore Professor of Music. Sinta may be heard on the CD releases of William Walton's *Façade* with the Lincoln Center Chamber Players and George Crumb's *Quest* with Speculum Musicale of New York City. Sinta is the Earl V. Moore Professor of Music.

Smith, Glenn: *Trombone.* Smith had an early background in classroom teaching in the public schools of Kansas and Illinois and was professor of trombone at the University of Michigan. He proceeded with specialization in each level of a student's progress through junior college age and added the artist level through his association as assistant principal trombone in the Chicago Civic Orchestra—the training orchestra sponsored by the Chicago Symphony.

His fine specialization at each level of trombone pedagogy made him a teacher *par excellence*. Over the years, Smith published thirty articles of a pedagogic nature that played their part in lifting knowledge and teaching skills for the trombone. His fine organization and clarity of expression made him sought after by the teaching profession. His articles appeared in journals published by brass manufacturers such as the Holton *Fanfare* and especially the *ITA Journal* published at North Texas State University in Denton. Smith was honored for his teaching expertise at the ITA International Conference in Cleveland in 1995.

Stout, Glennis: *Flute.* A soloist, lecturer, and adjudicator, Stout performed in Ann Arbor for some thirty-five years. Her special interest is centered in a formidable collection of historic flutes she uses in her demonstration lectures. As a Fulbright Scholar, her project is to pursue her studies and interests in this field of music expertise in Taiwan. Stout was principal flutist of the Plymouth (Michigan) Symphony and was formerly the editor of the *Flutist Quarterly*.

Stout, Louis J.: *French horn.* While Louis Stout's performing career, including five years with the Chicago Symphony, was undeniably distinguished, it is his contribution to music through the legacy of fine students for which he is universally lauded. In 1960, Stout applied for the position of horn instructor at the University of Michigan, armed with the confidence of being offered every position for which he had auditioned. He indeed got the job and remained there for twenty-eight years, annually turning out fine French horn players. "I've got ninety students playing professionally," he rightly boasts. "I don't think any other teacher comes close."

Stout's interest in the horn has led to the acquisition of a vast collection, regarded as one of the finest in the world. It is now housed at the Schloss Kremsegg Museum located in Kremsmünster, Austria. Lately, Louis maintained an active roster of private students.

Titiev, Estelle: *Piano.* Titiev earned a degree in performance and accompanying from the Cleveland Institute of Music. She accompanied and toured with all the first chair members of the Cleveland Orchestra and the renowned singers of her time, as well as having a solo piano career. She served on the Board of Directors of the Ann Arbor Symphony Orchestra and was listed as an honorary life member in 1986. Titiev also taught privately.

Webster, Michael: *Clarinet.* A multi-faceted musician, Michael Webster is known as clarinetist, conductor, composer, arranger, and pedagogue. Professor of clarinet and ensembles at Rice University's Shepherd School of Music in Houston, he is also Artistic Director of the Houston Youth Symphony. Formerly principal clarinetist with the Rochester Philharmonic and the San Francisco Symphony, he has appeared as a soloist with many orchestras, including the Philadelphia Orchestra and the Boston Pops. He has performed with the Chamber Music Society of Lincoln Center, the 92nd Street Y, Da Camera of Houston, the Tokyo, Cleveland, Muir, Ying, Leontóvych, and Chester String Quartets, and the festivals of Marlboro, Santa Fe, Chamber Music West and Northwest, Norfolk, Victoria, Stratford, Domaine Forget, Angel Fire, Steamboat Springs, Park City, Sitka, Skaneateles, and La Musica di Asolo.

In Rochester, Webster directed the Society for Chamber Music for eleven years and taught at the Eastman School, from which he earned three degrees. He was a member of the conducting faculty of the New England Conservatory and taught clarinet both there and at Boston University. He served as Music Director of the Wellesley Symphony Orchestra and guest conducted several Boston-area orchestras before becoming an adjunct professor of conducting at the University of Michigan.

He is the founder and director emeritus of Chamber Music Ann Arbor, which presents SpringFest every May. With his wife, flutist Leone Buyse, and pianist Robert Moeling he plays in the Webster Trio, which has released *Tour de France* and *WorldWideWebster* on Crystal Records. As a composer and arranger, he has been published by G. Schirmer and International, and he is recorded by C.R.I., Crystal, and Nami (Japan). Highly regarded as a pedagogue, he is a member of the editorial staff of *The Clarinet* magazine, contributing a regular column entitled "Teaching Clarinet."

Acknowledgments

GIA Publications and Rebecca Ericsson Hunter would like to express their gratitude to the many people, named and unnamed, who contributed to the publication of *Practicing Successfully: A Masterclass in the Musical Art* by Elizabeth A. H. Green.

Special thanks go to E. Daniel Long and H. Robert Reynolds for sharing their perspectives on the exceptional musicianship and personality of Elizabeth Green.

Thanks also go to Bob Phillips, a student in Elizabeth A. H. Green's last class at the University of Michigan who brought this book to GIA's attention. He writes, "String teacher Dan Long mentioned it to me over dinner and, as a string editor at Alfred Publishing, my ears perked up. I then made a trip to visit Michael Avsharian at Shar Products, who had the only copy in existence. Michael generously allowed me to take the manuscript with me. Upon reading it and contacting Rebecca Hunter, I was determined to find a publisher. After much research, I decided GIA was the perfect home for this important work and was very pleased when the decision was made to publish it. On behalf of all Miss Green's former students, I would like to say thank you to Alec Harris and everyone at GIA for completing this wonderful work."

Our gratitude goes to the noted experts Leone Buyse, L. Hugh Cooper, Lawrence Hurst, Fritz Kaenzig, Paul Kantor, Glennis Stout, Louis Stout, and Michael Webster for updating their pedagogical recommendations for factual accuracy and currency. Mary Steffek Blaske, executive director of the Ann Arbor Symphony Orchestra, and David Smith were helpful in fact-checking the manuscript.

We would also like to express appreciation to the Bentley Historical Library for access to photographic documents and to Charles Reynolds, music librarian at the University of Michigan, for his careful research.

BIBLIOGRAPHY

Chao, Mei-po. *The Yellow Bell: A Brief Sketch of the History of Chinese Music*. Baldwin, MD: Private Publication, 1934.

Cooper, L. Hugh. *Essentials of Bassoon Technique (German System) Based on the Performance Principles of Lewis Hugh Cooper*. Union, NJ: H. Toplansky, 1968.

Czerny, Carl. *The Art of Finger Dexterity*, Op. 740. New York: G. Schirmer, 1986.

Galamian, Ivan. *Principles of Violin Playing and Teaching*. Third Edition. Ann Arbor, MI: Shar Products Co., 1999.

Gaviniès, Pierre. *Twenty-four Studies for the Violin*. Augener, Ltd.: London, 1917.

Green, Elizabeth A. H. *Orchestral Bowings and Routines*. Bryn Mawr, PA: American String Teachers Association, 1949.

Kreutzer, Rodolphe. *Forty-two Etudes*. M. Senart & Cie: Paris, 1915.

Lillya, Clifford P. *Method for Cornet and Trumpet*. Chicago: M. M. Cole, 1937.

————. *Trumpet (Cornet) Technic: A Summary of Basic Skills, Applied Music Theory, Orchestra and Band Routine, Recital and Chamber Music Literature*. Rev. ed. Montrose, CA: Balquhidder Music, 1995.

Maier, Guy. "The Teacher's Round Table." *The Etude*. Theodore Presser Co. (magazine published 1883–1957)

Rigden, John S. *Physics and the Sound of Music*. New York: Wiley, 1977.
Taylor, Charles Alfred. *Exploring Music: The Science and Technology of Tones and Tunes*. Philadelphia: Institute of Physics Publishing, 1992.

Trott, Josephine. *Melodious Double-Stops*, Books 1 and 2. New York: Schirmer Books, 1986.

Wilson, Frank R. *Tone Deaf and All Thumbs? An Invitation to Music Making for Late Bloomers and Non-Prodigies*. New York: Viking, 1986.

About the Author

Elizabeth A. H. Green has been recognized as one of the most important and highly esteemed teachers of stringed instruments and conducting in America. Her books are used in classrooms of major universities, and her associations with some of the greatest violinists and conductors in the world put her in high demand as a lecturer.

Her compositions include *Chatterbox Symphonette* (1950), Theme and Variations (1960), Twelve Modern Etudes for Advanced Violinists (1964), and Sinfonia in D (by Johann Stamitz, arranged by Elizabeth Green for string orchestra in 1970). Some of her scholarly publications are: *Orchestral Bowings and Routines, Musicianship, Repertoire for the High School Orchestra, Teaching String Instruments in Classes, Increasing the Proficiency on the Violin, The Dynamic Orchestra,* and *The Modern Conductor* (now in its seventh edition).

Green received her bachelor of science degree from Wheaton College (Illinois) and was the founding member of the symphony orchestra in Waterloo, Iowa. She received her master's degree from Northwestern University in 1939. She studied violin from 1947–1955 with Ivan Galamian at the Meadowmount Music School. With Green's help, Galamian set down his violin philosophy in the 1961 book *Principles of Violin Playing.*

In 1993, Green published a biography of her former instructor entitled *Miraculous Teacher: Ivan Galamian and the Meadowmount Experience.* Green also studied violin under Jacques Gordon at the Chicago Symphony Orchestra and at Music Mountain in Connecticut.

She studied the viola with Clarence Evans, principal violist of the Chicago Symphony from 1929–1930. It was on the recommendations of these teachers that Green studied conducting with Nicolai Malko, a Russian composer whose teaching philosophy was the basis of *The Modern Conductor*, a standard conducting text in the field today.

Green completed Malko's *The Conductor and His Score*, which was published in 1975. She once served as a judge in the prestigious Nicolai Malko Competition, which is held every three years in Copenhagen. Upon retiring from the University of Michigan after thirty-two years of teaching in 1975, Green enrolled at Eastern Michigan University, where she studied painting. In 1978, she was awarded a bachelor's degree in art.

In March 1995, Elizabeth Green was honored by the Michigan House of Representatives by resolution as a world-famous educator, musician, author, and conductor. She was awarded the American String Teachers Association Distinguished Service Award, and the association has presented the Elizabeth A. H. Green School Educator Award since 1990. She was inducted into the Women Band Directors International Hall of Fame of Distinguished Conductors in 2000. She has also received commendations from Northwestern University, the Midwest Band and Orchestra Clinic, Tau Beta Sigma, Phi Beta Mu, Wheaton College, and the University of Michigan.

Green died of cancer on September 24, 1995, at her home in Ann Arbor at the age of 89.

Comprehensive Index

alto clarinet 92
alto clef 111
alto saxophone 93
Art of Finger Dexterity, The (Czerny) 60
artificial harmonics 108

Ballet Suite, "Gigue" (Gretry) 31
baritone saxophone 93
bass clarinet 92
bass saxophone 93
bassethorn 92
bassoon 93–95
Beethoven, Ludwig van 35
Berezovsky, Boris 74
Bloom, Robert 90
Boulanger, Nadia 45
bowing 30, 38–39, 45, 59, 69, 79, 82, 109–110
brass instruments 97–104
Buyse, Leone 88–89, 131

Cassavant, A. R. 127
cello 43–45, 70, 79–81, 106–108, 112
changes in dynamics 61
chord of nature 74
chords 82–83
clarinet 91–92
Concertino da Camera (Ibert) 93
Concerto for Clarinet and Orchestra in A, op. 57 (Nielsen) 22
Concerto for Saxophone and Orchestra (Glazunov) 93
Cooper, L. Hugh 93, 128, 132
cornet 99–101
cross accentuation 41–43, 45, 60
Csikszentmihalyi, Dr. Mihaly 121
Czerny, Carl 33, 40, 60

d'Arezzo, Guido 67
Dahl, Ingolf 93
damper pedal 73, 76
Debost, Michel 89
Debussy, Claude 26
Der Freischütz Overture 105

Dick, Robert 89
dotted-eighth sixteenth 20–23, 31, 33
double bass 107
double-stops 79–82
dynamic control 29

E-flat soprano clarinet 92
etude 59–63
Etude, The 65
euphonium 103
Evans, Clarence 66

Fantasia Appasionata, op. 35 (Vieuxtemps) 28
fermata-rest 23–25, 30, 63, 83, 94, 118
fingering system 106
flugelhorn 101
flute 87–89
flutter pedaling 78
Forty-two Etudes 59
Francesca da Rimini, op. 32 (Tchaikovsky) 26
French bow 112–113
French horn 97–99

Galamian, Ivan 51–52, 80, 108, 110, 119
Gaviniès, Pierre 60, 62
German bow 112–114
Gingold, Joseph 112
glorification of discord 57
Gretry, André 31

harmonics 108
harp 32, 105–106
human brain 117
Hurst, Lawrence 129, 132
Husa, Karel 93

Kaenzig, Fritz 103–104, 133
Kantor, Paul 128, 134
Kovar, Simon 94
Kreutzer, Rodolphe 59
Kuhlau, Friedrich 48
La bohème (Puccini) 105

La mer (Debussy) 26
learning to practice 122–129
left brain 117
legato tonguing 101–102
Lillya, Clifford 99, 134
lip slur 98–102

Maier, Guy 65
memory 128–129
Method for Cornet and Trumpet (Lillya)
  99–100
modern innovations 55, 57
Mottl, Felix 31
Moyse, Marcel 89
Mussorgsky, Modest 26

neural pathway 118
Nielsen, Carl 22
note-repetition studies 43

oboe 89–91
Op. 740, Etude no. 2 (Czerny) 33
Op. 740, Etude no. 5 (Czerny) 40
Orchestral Bowings and Routines (Green)
  67–68
overtone series 78, 97, 102

pedaling 76
piano 32–33, 62, 66, 73–78
Pictures at an Exhibition, "The Great Gate
  of Kiev" (Mussorgsky) 26
pizzicato 105–106, 114
practicing in fours 35–36, 39–40, 43
practicing in threes 27–33, 50
practicing sequences 47
Principles of Violin Playing and Teaching
  (Galamian) 119
Puccini, Giacomo 105

Rasher, Sigurd 93
Ravel, Maurice 26
reiteration of fourths 57
reiteration of major sevenths 57
repeated notes 61
rhythmic motif 20–25, 28–33, 35–36,
  39–41, 60
rhythmic subdivision 56
Rigden, John S. 75

right brain 117
Rondo, op. 20, no. 1 (Kuhlau) 48

Sargous, Harry 90, 135
Sax, Adolphe 92
saxophone 92–93
scale 48–53
scratch tone 82
seven positions 107
seventh partial 102
sight-reading 65–69, 71
Sinta, Donald 92, 135
Smith, Glenn 101, 135
Solti, Georg 129
soprano cornet 99
soprano saxophone 93
Squire, William 28
Stout, Glennis 88, 136
Stout, Louis J. 98, 104, 136
string bass 43–45, 70, 79–81, 106–108,
  112, 114
string crossings 63, 82–83
strings 29, 38–39, 43–44, 62–63, 70,
  79–81, 83, 105–111, 114, 126
substitution accents 47–49
sustaining pedal 73–74, 77
switching from violin to viola 110
sympathetic vibration 76–78
Symphony no. 4, Fourth Movement
  (Beethoven) 35
Symphony no. 5, op. 64 (Tchaikovsky)
  30

Tarantella, op. 23 (Squire) 28
Taylor, Charles 75
Tchaikovsky, Piotr 26, 30
tenor saxophone 93
"The Flow" 121
time counting chart for the beginner 68
Titiev, Estelle 75, 136
Torello, Anton Sr. 114
touch 75
trombone 101–102
trumpet 99–101
tuba 103–104
two-note slur 42

unity of the beat 69

Vieuxtemps, Henri   28
viola clef   111
viola   43–45, 69–70, 79–81, 83, 106–112
violin   43–45, 69–70, 79–81, 83, 106–111
von Weber, Carl Maria   105

Webster, Michael   91, 137
winds   29, 70
woodwinds   87–91, 93–95

Yellow Bell, The   87, 95

Zukerman, Pinchas   112